Fatima
Revealed . . .

. . . **and Discarded**

Fatima
Revealed . . .
. . . and Discarded

BROTHER MICHEL DE LA SAINTE TRINITE

Translated from the French by
Timothy Tindal-Robertson

DEVON, MCMLXXXVIII

©Augustine Publishing Company, 1988

©Frère Michel de la Sainte Trinité, 1988
(original French language edition)

©T.Tindal-Robertson, 1988
(English language translation)

ISBN 0 85172 749 2

PUBLISHER'S NOTICE

This edition comprises a selection of extracts from the 3-volume history of Fatima by Frère Michel de la Sainte Trinité, entitled *Toute la Vérité sur Fatima*. It is published with the agreement of the author, and the selection, editing and translation has been carried out by T.Tindal-Robertson.

The author hopes to publish next in the French a single volume in abbreviation of the three volumes which he has published so far, and thereafter to complete the series with Volume IV, which will cover the developments with regard to Fatima from 1960 onwards.

Typeset by Sandra A.Daniels,

Printed and bound by Cox & Wyman Ltd., Reading,

and published March 1988 by
AUGUSTINE PUBLISHING COMPANY,
CHULMLEIGH, DEVON EX18 7HL

CONTENTS

Part I : Fatima Revealed

responds to the grace of Fatima - 13 May 1931, national consecration of Portual to the Immaculate Heart of Mary

The miraculous spiritual conversion - The miraculous social and political renewal - The miraculous preservation of Portugal from the scourge of the Spanish Civil War and World War 2

Our Lord complains to Sr. Lucia about laxity of life in Spain, and threatens further Soviet chastisement - The positive response of the bishops of Portugal and Spain - Spain eventually spared further chastisement

Aug. 1931, Our Lord's communication to Sr. Lucia at Rianjo - the historical significance of His reference to Paray-le-Monial - 17 June, 1789, the French Catholic monarchy dissolved 100 years later to the day on which Our Lord conveyed His designs to St. Margaret Mary

1942, notable events of the 25th Fatima Jubilee year - First publication of the great Secret - 1943, consecration of the world to the Immaculate Heart of Mary - The 'Great Return' in France - 1944, Feast of the Immaculate Heart of Mary - 1945-46, increasing devotion to Mary; Pius XII broadcasts to Portugal for the coronation of Our Lady of Fatima - The miracle of the doves

Part II : Fatima Discarded

miracle of the sun in the Vatican gardens - The
definition of the dogma of the Assumption - The Pope's
vision a sign from Our Lady for him to fulfill her
requests - Pius XII remains undecided - Oct. 1951,
International Congress on the Message of Fatima at
Lisbon, and broadcast of Pius XII for the close of the
Holy Year

has read it, states that it contains three elements: "the dangers threatening the faith", "the importance of the last times", and the fact that the prophecies "contained in this Third Secret correspond to what Scripture announces".

Bibliography

ILLUSTRATIONS

Chapter I

PORTUGAL, "LAND OF HOLY MARY"

In her Memoirs, Lucia tells us that Jacinta was very fond of singing to pass away the long hours of solitude while the three shepherd children of Aljustrel were looking after their sheep. One of their favourite songs, the 'Salve Nobre Padroeira', which was very popular in Portugal, runs:

"Hail, O noble Patron.
Of the people whom you protect,
Of the people chosen among all others
As the people of the Lord!

O Thou, glory of our land,
Whom you have saved a thousand times!
As long as there will be Portuguese people
You will always be their love!"
(Fr. Joao de Marchi, I.M.C., *Temoignages sur les Apparitions de Fatima*, 1979, p.66).

This song evokes the marvellous history of a nation entirely devoted to the Immaculate Virgin from its very beginnings. Eight years after the solemn consecration of France to Our Lady by King Louis XIII, Portugal was officially consecrated to the Immaculate Virgin in 1646 by King John IV, the restorer of national independence. By an admirable grace of predilection, which flowed from its national vocation, Portugal had long been prepared to receive the Queen of Heaven. We have only space here to describe the most outstanding episodes in this admirable alliance, which was forged so early on in the country's history, so often renewed and never broken, and which made this happy country, long before the Virgin of the Rosary came there to Fatima, the "Land of Holy Mary".

The former Roman Province of Lusitania was evangelised at an early date, but in the year 711 the Moors invaded the country, which had to wait nearly three centuries for the dawning of its deliverance. The French crusaders, who were called to its help in 1086 by King Alfonsus VI, King of Castille and Leon, were to play a leading role in its glorious reconquest. In 1095, Henry, son of the Duke of Burgundy, had liberated the whole of the northern part of the country, between Minho and Douro, from the Moslem yoke. This feat won him the hand of the daughter of the King of Castille and the possession of the whole of the region he had conquered, under the title of Count of Portugal. As the nephew of the great Saint Hugh, the powerful abbot of Cluny, Henry encouraged the foundation of several branches of the French abbey. The first two archbishops of Braga were both French Cluniac monks.

But it was his son, Alfonso Henriques, who consolidated the independence of Portugal by his victory in 1139 at Ourica over the Moors. His soldiers, who were for the most part French crusaders, proclaimed him king on the field of battle. When his overlord, the King of Castille, protested against this usurpation, Henriques demanded and obtained the protection of Pope Innocent II as his overlord.

However, most important of all, the new king immediately chose the Mother of God as the patron of his country and of his new dynasty. "The founder of the kingdom," writes the Portuguese historian, Father Oliveira Dias, "placed it under the protection of Mary, naming her as the Protectress and Mother of all the Portuguese, and at the same time he decreed that an annual tribute should be paid to the Church of Saint Mary of Clairvaux, in the name of its abbot, Saint Bernard, and his successors. The document recording this gift, which was signed in the cathedral of Lamego on 28 April 1142, was found in the monastery of Alcobaca, written on parchment and stamped with the royal seal."

The Cistercians began to arrive in Portugal in 1140, and were destined to have an immense influence on the young kingdom, developing among the people a deep devotion to Our Lady. In 1142 King Alfonso Henriques gave to St. Bernard the land on which was built, only a short distance from Fatima, the magnificent monastery of Alcobaca. When he was planning his audacious conquest of Santarem, which at that time was in the hands of the Moors, the King made a vow to build a monastery consecrated to the Virgin, if he was victorious in battle. This is how he came to build the monastery of Santa Maria of Alcobaca. Thereafter, the crusaders used to carry into battle with them a statue of Our Lady, which was venerated until the eighteenth century in the church of Our Lady of Martyrs in Lisbon. All the conquests of King Alfonso Henriques, the founder of the nation, were undertaken and brought to pass under the auspices of Our Lady, remarks Father Oliveira Dias.

Here it is appropriate to remark, if we may believe the words of an ancient ballad, that it is to an episode in the reconquest of Portugal about this time that Fatima owes its Arabic name. Fatima, the daughter of a powerful Moslem prince, Alacer do Sol, was captured by a crusader, Goncalo Hermingues. When the Christian knight asked the prince for his daughter's hand in marriage, she converted and was baptised as Ouranea, from which the nearby town of Ourem took its name. But the beautiful princess died in her youth, and Don Goncalo Hermingues, in his distress, gave up his life to God in the Cistercian abbey of Alcobaca. A little later, the abbey founded a small priory in the neighbouring mountain; Brother Goncalo was sent there and took with him the remains of his dear Fatima. The place took and kept her name.

It is at the same period that the Sanctuary of Our Lady of Nazaré was founded, which was to remain so popular for many centuries.

Is there any other nation whose foundation is so closely linked to the cult and devotion of the Virgin Mary?

As the result of dynastic troubles, by 1383 Castille again dominated Portugal. The instrument of the country's miraculous deliverance this time was Blessed Dom Nuno Alvares Pereira, a man with a great devotion to Our Lady. While the King was still hesitating in front of the more numerous Castillian army, Dom Nuno decided to march alone into battle. The image of the Virgin was embroidered on his standard and his troops were given the war-cry "In the name of God and of the Virgin Mary!" On 13 August 1385, before meeting the more powerful army of the King of Castille, he drew up his troops on the plateau at Fatima, where the King of Portugal finally rejoined him. There they both solemnly invoked the protection of Mary, and the King knelt down before her image and vowed that if the victory was given to him, he would build a beautiful monastery in her honour, and make a pilgrimage of thanksgiving to the Sanctuary of Our Lady of Oliveira.

This was the first "thirteenth" day of the month celebrated in honour of Our Lady in this land chosen by her. The following day, on the vigil of the Assumption, the great victory of Aljubarrota assured the independence of the country for two centuries. In his bull of February 1391, Pope Boniface IX unhesitatingly described the victory as miraculous, such had been the crushing superiority of the Spanish forces. "In fulfilment of his vow, the King hastened to construct the church and monastery of Batalha, a real poem of stone, a magnificent jewel of different styles and an immortal monument to Portugal's recognition of the Virgin Mary. He gave it the name of Our Lady of Victory," writes the Portuguese historian, Father Oliveira Dias. From this

Dominican monastery, the devotion to the holy Rosary spread throughout the country.

Is it not remarkable that the two most outstanding monuments to Portugal's national independence — Alcobaca and Batalha — were both built to the glory of the Virgin Mary, and were situated only a short distance from Fatima?

It is also worth noting that Blessed Nuno Pereira was Count of Ourem and Lord of the region of Fatima. In recognition for all the victories which Our Lady had granted the Portuguese, he built in her honour the great convent of the Carmelites at Lisbon, whose six chapels are all dedicated to the Mother of God under different titles, and he also built six other churches in honour of the Virgin.

For two centuries Portugal was to rise to the height of its power, with crusades, great maritime discoveries, missionary labours and the foundation of colonies. But in 1580, on the death of the Cardinal-King, Portugal lost its national monarchy and fell under Spanish domination for a second time. However, this new decline was the occasion for the solemn renewal of its ancient alliance with the Virgin Mary.

In 1638, King Louis XIII of France had consecrated "his person, his State, his crown and his subjects, to the most holy and glorious Virgin, as special protectress of his kingdom". This act aroused a great movement of fervour in France, and King John IV of Portugal decided to follow the example of Louis XIII. On 20 October 1646, "as a sign of love and recognition, he laid down his royal crown at the feet of Our Lady of the Immaculate Conception. With all his nation reunited in the Cortes, he proclaimed her Patron of his kingdom, 'hoping with great confidence in the infinite mercy of Our Lord, who, by the intermediary of this Patron and Protectress of our kingdoms and our lands of which we have the honour to declare ourselves her vassals and tributaries, will protect and defend us against our

enemies while considerably increasing our lands, for the
glory of Christ Our God and for the exaltation of the
holy Roman Catholic faith, the conversion of pagans and
the submission of heretics' ".

By this solemn act, Portugal, faithful to its own
tradition, chose to consecrate itself to the Virgin Mary
under the title of her Immaculate Conception, preceding
by two centuries the infallible definition of Pope Pius
IX.   Father Oliveira Dias observes that the pious
monarch took an oath, to which the heir apparent and
the Cortes also bound themselves, to propose and defend
even at the cost of his life the doctrine of the Immaculate
Conception of Mary, and the words of this vow are so
admirable that we cannot omit to quote the following
extract from it:

"And if anyone dares to attempt anything whatever
against our promise, oath and vassalage, we consider
him from this moment as no longer belonging to the
nation and we wish that he should be driven out of the
kingdom; and if he is king, which may God prevent,
may the divine malediction and ours fall on him and may
he no longer be counted among our descendants;   we
solemnly vow that he should be thrown down and
stripped of the throne by the same God who gave us the
kingdom and raised us to the royal dignity."

(Father Oliveira Dias, S.J., article in *Maria, Etudes sur
la Sainte Vierge, 1956*, vol.4, p.624).

In order to underline and perpetuate the national
character of his vow, the King ordered that an
inscription should be carved in marble or some other
stone above the gates of towns, recalling this oath of the
King and of the Cortes in honour of the Mother of God
"preserved from original sin".   Apparently, one of these
inscriptions may still be seen on a property at Leiria in
Alcobaca Street.

Here we are right at the heart of the mystery of the
words which the Blessed Virgin was to speak to Lucia
nearly three centuries later: "In Portugal the dogma of

the faith will always be preserved." For while the text of
the solemn vow above the gates of the towns, to defend
forever the dogma of the Immaculate Conception, was
broken up by the liberal governments of the nineteenth
century or by the revolutionaries of 1910, the Virgin
Mary herself did not forget it, and it is her most faithful
nation which she chose in order to manifest to the world
the mercy of her Immaculate Heart.

To perpetuate the memory of his vow, the King also
ordered medals in gold and silver to be struck, bearing
the effigy of the Immaculate Virgin "tutelaris regni",
"Protectress of the Kingdom". Finally, by royal letters,
the King ordered all the municipalities and the whole
clergy to take the Immaculate Virgin as Patron,
according to the form in the brief of Pope Urban VIII
which regulates the election of patron saints.

Was there any other nation in the world better
prepared to receive the great message of the Immaculate
Heart of Mary?

In the next two centuries, the dark clouds of
liberalism invaded the "Land of Holy Mary", but the
good people nevertheless remained faithful to their
heavenly Patron. In their enthusiasm for the definition
of the dogma of the Immaculate Conception in 1854, the
faithful raised to the glory of their Immaculate Queen
the superb national sanctuary of Sameiro near Braga.
The works were begun in 1863 and a magnificent statue
of the Immaculate was sculpted at Rome and blessed by
Pope Pius IX himself; Jacinta told Dr. Lisboa that this
was the image which most recalled to her mind the
Virgin such as she had contemplated her at Fatima.

Of the foreign pilgrims to Lourdes, the Portuguese
were without doubt the first, the most numerous and the
most fervent to come in groups, accompanied by their
priests, their bishops, and their archbishops. In 1876,
the patriarch of Lisbon went to the grotto, and two years
later King Fernando visited it with several members of
his family. Soon, the Portuguese were frequenting

Lourdes in their thousands, and after the revolution of
1910 many exiles chose to live in the Marian town which
was so dear to them.

Finally, according to Canon Galamba it was the
region of Fatima which remained the most loyal to the
Church. "The neighbourhood of Ourem in which Fatima
is situated was well known for the generosity of its
inhabitants, the number of its priests and the abundance
of its vocations... Its priests and faithful could be relied
upon in no matter what circumstances...   In this
agitated period (in 1911, after the law of the separation
of the Church and the State), they were never able to
take an inventory of the goods of the Church, and to my
knowledge this was absolutely unique in all Portugal.
The clergy and the faithful were a formidable force."
(Canon Galamba: *Fatima a Prova*, pp. 25-27).

So it was indeed in truth that the three little
shepherds could sing the beautiful traditional refrain, as
they kept their sheep:

"Hail, O noble Patron
Of the people whom you protect,
Of the people chosen among all others
As the people of the Lord!

O Thou, glory of our land,
Whom you have saved a thousand times!
As long as there will be Portuguese people
You will always be their love!"

Chapter II

PORTUGAL BEFORE AND AFTER FATIMA

In order to understand the reality and the extent of the miraculous and saving intervention of heaven which took place in Portugal in 1917, let us recall first of all just how far the forces of evil had succeeded in leading the country right up to the edge of the abyss. When the Angel of Portugal, its guardian angel, came to invite the three little shepherds of Aljustrel to sacrifice themselves for the peace of their country in the summer of 1916, it was indeed in a very sorry and pitiful condition.

The economic collapse, which had been recently aggravated by Portugal's entry into the war, disorder and anarchy, strife and murders, and the outrages which had become commonplace - all these created a veritable climate of civil war. The Church had been banished from society, and was reduced to silence and persecuted in all sorts of ways. Seeing the country in such a state, who would have been able to believe that only one year later the dawn of its salvation would be in sight; that it would soon enjoy perfect peace, and that the Church, marvellously restored, would recover its radiance and fervour of past centuries?

Such an event was completely unforseeable, and that it took place at all was due purely to the miraculous intervention of the most powerful Virgin Mary, the Immaculate Mediatrix, who thus accomplished in six months on behalf of her faithful nation something which neither the monarchy nor the Church had succeeded in bringing about for more than a century.

In the eighteenth century, José de Carvalho, Marquis of Pombal, who was a notorious Freemason, engaged in an open and brutal war against the Church. In

September 1759, Pombal compelled the King to sign an edict expelling the Jesuits from all his states. Pombal's agents even travelled as far as the missions in China, India, the Congo, and Brazil, in order to remove them. In the course of these brutal expulsions, not less than 270 religious died for their faith.

By expelling the Jesuits Pombal had struck at the heart of the Church in Portugal. Their departure left the Church defenceless against the crude anti-clerical propaganda which swept the country. After a brief Catholic restoration, the French Revolution brought a renewed period of trouble to the country. During the nineteenth century, the Catholic monarchy steadily lost ground against the rising influence of the anti-clerical and revolutionary parties, aided by the intrigues of the Freemasons.

Finally, on 1 February 1908, two carbonari assassinated the King and his son, the heir apparent, and eventually a Republic was proclaimed on 5 October 1910. The revolution inaugurated a period of ferocious persecution of the Church. Although the country was at that time in a disastrous economic situation, it was their violently anti-religious policy which occupied the whole attention of the provisional government. Only five days after the Republic had been installed, a decree was published re-imposing all the laws of Pombal and Aguiar: all the convents, monasteries and establishments of all religious orders of whatever denomination were suppressed, all their religious members were expelled and all their goods were confiscated. The Jesuits were declared to have forfeited their Portuguese nationality.

From then on, there was a flood of anti-religious decrees and legislation: divorce, cremation, the secularization of cemeteries, the abolition of the religious oath, the suppression of religious teaching in schools, the prohibition on wearing the cassock – nothing was overlooked. The public celebration of religious feasts was suppressed, the State demanded the right to nominate the professors and to determine the programmes at seminaries, and so on.

All these persecuting measures finally culminated in the law of the separation of the Church and State, which was voted on 20 April 1911. The author of these laws, one Alfonso Costa, declared about this time: "thanks to this law of separation, in two generations Catholicism will be completely eliminated from Portugal." But he spoke without taking into account the clear-sightedness and the firmness of the Pope, St. Pius X, and the protection of Portugal's heavenly Patron. Barely one month later, on 24 May 1911, feast of Our Lady, Help of Christians, the Pope issued an encyclical entitled *Jamdudum in Lusitania*, in which he firmly condemned "the very bad and pernicious law of the separation of the Church and the State" and denounced "its monstrous absurdity", and its outrageous attempt to reduce the Church to "an odious servitude": "We reprove, condemn and reject the law on the separation of the Portuguese Republic and the Church: a law which despises God and repudiates the Catholic faith... We raise a solemn protest against its authors and against all those who have taken any part in it. We declare and denounce as null and without validity everything which this law has decreed contrary to the intangible rights of the Church," wrote the Pope in the encyclical.

Confronted with the unforeseen resistance of the hierarchy, the government resorted to banishment. Most of the bishops of the country were exiled, including the patriarch of Lisbon, the archbishops of Braga and Evora, the bishops of Porto and Viseu, and many others. Many priests were imprisoned, including Father José da Silva, the future bishop of Leiria.

The Portuguese historian, Canon Formigao, wrote of this period: "Matters which were already bad when the Republic was inaugurated, became immeasurably worst during the first years of the new regime: it was a period of utter persecution of the Church and dissolution of morals". Costa Brochado relates that in 1917 alone 69 churches and chapels were pillaged in the provinces and 42 in Lisbon, and in most cases the sacred species were profaned.

The apparitions of the Virgin at Fatima in 1917, at a time when Portugal was utterly prostrate under an accumulation of evils, was thus the occasion of a truly dramatic about-turn in the fortunes of the country. Less than fifteen years after the marvellous event, on 13 May 1931, in the name of the whole Portuguese Episcopate, and in the middle of a crowd of some 300,000 people, Cardinal Cerejeira gave thanks to the Virgin Mary for the miracle which She had accomplished: "Our Lady of Fatima, you have deigned to come down to our land, as a sign of blessing, announcing, like the morning star, the dawn of light and hope after the darkness of night" (Cardinal Cerejeira, *Obras Pastorais,* vol. 1, p.289).

That indeed is precisely what had happened. Even if the social and political revival did not immediately follow on the profusion of supernatural graces which Our Lady showered on the Cova da Iria, as from 13 May 1917 everything was soon to change in the hearts and souls of the faithful. When they learnt that the Virgin Mary herself, their queen and their mother, their heavenly protectress, had deigned to visit them, hope was rekindled at one stroke, and with it the certainty of victory over their persecutors.

Already, by 13 July, three or four thousand people had been attracted to the Cova da Iria. The stories of atmospheric prodigies and the announcement of a forthcoming miracle drew an increasing number of pilgrims from month to month. On 13 August, between eighteen and twenty thousand people came; on 13 September there were nearly thirty thousand, and for 13 October, some seventy thousand pilgrims had come from all over Portugal to assist at the miracle which had been promised. Confronted with this great popular movement of faith and devotion, the authorities and enemies of religion were powerless, unable to do anything, and not knowing what to do. The bonds of the cruel tyranny were already beginning to weaken.

The day after the great miracle of the sun on 13 October 1917 was a Sunday, and the date of the municipal elections. Comparing the results with the elections in 1911, the newspaper *O Dia* reported that the three main democratic, republican and evolutionist parties had lost 95,000 votes to the Catholics in the capital alone. Furious at this setback, some fanatical Freemasons decided to ransack the place of the apparitions, and on the night of 22 and 23 October they demolished the primitive sanctuary which had been erected at the Cova da Iria. They also mistakenly removed the wrong holm-oak tree on which they thought Our Lady had appeared. When she found out about this incident next day, Lucia wrote in her Memoirs that she "asked pardon of Our Lady for these poor men and prayed for their conversion".

The effect on public opinion produced by this outrage was absolutely contrary to what its authors intended. Even the anti-clerical press condemned it. The editor of *O Seculo* concluded "What a disgrace! How can the authorities possibly allow this sort of thing to take place and refuse permission for Catholic processions, while almost the entire population of Portugal belongs to the Church, and its processions do not offend the convictions of others in any way whatever?"

However, after seven years of violent and fanatical persecution, and after a whole century of being banned from society, as if by a miracle the Church was suddenly to recover the enjoyment of all those liberties to which she has a right, and which she needs in order to accomplish her work for the salvation of souls. What is so remarkable is that the man who put an end to this long situation of injustice – and with what decision and rapidity, since everything was completed within one year! – was no special friend of the Church.

A professor at Coimbra University and an officer in the army, Sidonio Pais had been the Portuguese ambassador at Berlin until March 1916, before becoming Minister of State. He was known to be a convinced Republican and affiliated to Freemasonry.

Having decided to put an end to the anarchy which was plunging his country into ruin, he led a coup d'état which brought him to power on precisely 8 December, (the date of the Feast of the Immaculate Conception), he decreed the dissolution of parliament, and he had himself nominated president of the Republic and head of the government by the revolutionary junta. One is astonished to find that this lifelong upper-class Freemason considered it as his most important and urgent task to reconcile the government with the Church. To the marvel of the Catholics, a completely new era began to open up.

The very day after his victory, Sidonio Pais removed all the measures which had been taken against the bishops, who were thus able to return to their country from exile. A whole succession of measures followed, repairing the wrongs which had been done to the Church by the revolution of 1910. On 28 June 1918, a communiqué announced the reconciliation of the Republic with Rome. On 4 July Sidonio Pais was congratulated by the Pope, and on the 10th a Portuguese legation was re-accredited to the Holy See, while Mgr. Locatelli was appointed apostolic nuncio at Lisbon.

However, it was when he began to prepare a law which was to restore their rights to the Society of Jesus that his former Masonic brethren decided he had gone too far. A first and unsuccessful attempt on his life was made on 6 December 1918. Eight days later, after attending a requiem Mass for sailors who had been killed in battle, he was shot in the railway station at Lisbon, and died on an operating table in the Saint Joseph hospital with a crucifix on his chest.

But the courageous head of state had not sacrificed his

life entirely in vain. Although after his assassination the country immediately subsided into political anarchy again, the republicans lacked the strength to reintroduce the anti-clerical laws. Owing to the work of Sidonio Pais, the persecutions had ceased, the Church had recovered her liberty, and despite a few further attempts to take it away from her again, henceforth she was to keep it.

Twenty years later, in a speech in which he recalled the tragic death of Sidonio Pais, Cardinal Cerejeira was able to declare: "Since Our Lady of Fatima appeared in 1917 in the sky above Portugal, a special blessing of God has come down on our land. The violent cycle of religious persecution has stopped, and a new era of peace between men and of Christian restoration has begun." (*Obras Pastorais*, vol. 1, pp. 142-144).

Chapter III

THE SECRET OF THE PILGRIMAGE

While the Church, as if by a miracle, had suddenly recovered her liberty of action, another miracle, less visible but certainly more important, secretly began to take effect in the hearts of the people. In the words of Father Paul Denis, O.P., "a new element had altered the whole situation, at first imperceptibly, then dazzlingly and decisively: after several centuries of lethargy, the Portuguese Church was recovering her self-confidence.

"This resurgence of confidence was due to the simple fact that the Catholics of Portugal, responding to the appeal of the Virgin, tirelessly went again and again on pilgrimage to Fatima. It was these enormous pulsations of a whole people which played an essential role in the religious uplifting of Portugal. Little by little the former inferiority complex was replaced by a proud and joyful assurance in the Church and in themselves" (Quoted by G. Renault, *Fatima*, p.218). Father Denis concludes that "only the new atmosphere created by Fatima made possible and relatively easy the work of political cleansing and national and social reconstruction..." (Op.cit., p.220).

Just as in the Gospel, for the most part it was the poor people, the peasants and inhabitants of the countryside, who were the first to hear the message from heaven. Maria Carreira is the most authoritative witness of those early days, and she told Father De Marchi:

"From the 13th October, the day when the sun danced in the sky, it was a continual procession, especially on Sundays and on the 13th of each month. There were local people, and others who had come a long distance. The men arrived with a stick, carrying their provisions on their backs; the women carried their children under their arms. There were even some old men who came and who seemed to have no strength left. They all knelt down near the holm-oak on which Our Lady had appeared. Nobody seemed to be disappointed, nobody seemed tired. There was absolutely nothing for sale, not even a glass of water or a glass of wine!

"How rich those times were in penance! It was enough to bring tears to your eyes!... When there were a large number of people present, they sang the beautiful hymns of the Church... They did much penance, and they did it with much joy. The people went home entirely content and satisfied. They came to ask Our Lady to work miracles for them, and Our Lady answered all their prayers. At that time, I never heard it said that Our Lady had refused a miracle to anyone. All those who came here came with devotion; or else, if they had no devotion when they came, they found it here." (De Marchi, *Temoignages*, pp.230-231).

About August 1918, they began the construction of a little chapel on the site of the apparitions, and in May 1920 a beautiful painted wooden statue, which had been carved by the young sculptor José Ferreira Thedim, was installed there. This statue soon became very dear to popular devotion. It was lightly touched up by the artist in 1951 or 1952, and is still venerated at the Capelinha today.

At the moment when the government was vainly considering how to oppose the development of the pilgrimage, an event of the greatest significance for the future of Fatima took place. On 15 May 1920, Pope Benedict XV finally appointed a bishop to the diocese of Leiria, which had been restored two years earlier. Mgr. José Correia da Silva was consecrated on 25 July in the cathedral of Porto, and took possession of his diocese on 5 August. The new bishop was a very cultured man, who had taught Church history, biblical science and theology at the seminary of Porto since 1897. He had

also been active in editing two Catholic papers and
engaged in various other Catholic social works; at the
time of the 1910 revolution he was arrested five times
and kept in prison for a total of eight months. He was
known for his profound piety and for his great love for
the Blessed Virgin. He had a special devotion for Our
Lady of Lourdes, where he had already been twelve
times on pilgrimage. On 15 August 1920, he solemnly
consecrated his diocese to the Virgin Mary. So what did
he think of the events at Fatima? He himself later told
Canon Barthas:

"I had never wanted to be concerned with it, to the
point – you will not believe this - that I did not even
know where Fatima was. It is just children's tales, I told
myself. When the apostolic nuncio asked me to consider
reconstituting the diocese of Leiria, I was very hesitant.
In the whole town of Leiria there was only one priest! To
encourage me, the bishop of Portalegre said to me: 'You
have Fatima in your diocese, a new Lourdes!' 'O!' I
replied 'yet another trouble'. In a word, I was
incredulous. Nevertheless, when I accepted the
responsibility, I resolved to wait for signs from divine
Providence which would guide my conduct" (Canon C.
Barthas, *Fatima 1917-1968*, pp. 257-258).

Finally, after a year spent listening to many people's
views, he reached his own conclusion, which was
resolutely in favour of the authenticity of the
apparitions. Accordingly in June 1921 he removed
Lucia from Aljustrel to continue her education in the
college of Vilar at Porto.

At the same time he decided to keep a watchful eye
on the spontaneous cult which had sprung up at the Cova
da Iria, without any control on the part of the clergy.
On 12 September 1921 he made his first visit to Fatima,
recited the rosary at the Capelinha, and met the peasants
of the locality, some of whom had already made him
gifts of the lands which they possessed at the Cova da
Iria and in the neighbourhood. At the same time the

faithful Maria Carreira was able to give him the considerable sum of the offerings of the faithful which she had kept since August 1917, and on 14 September the deeds recording the gift or sale of lands were signed in front of a notary.

13 October of that year was the fourth anniversary of the last apparition of Our Lady. With the permission of the bishop, the chapel was finally blessed and for the first time Mass was celebrated there. From then on, the bishop permitted the celebration of a low Mass with sermon on the days when the greatest crowds of pilgrims thronged to the Cova da Iria.

Meanwhile, an unexpected solution was found to the increasingly urgent problem of lack of water, which had been causing disputes between the local inhabitants and the pilgrims. In September, the bishop had asked Maria Carreira to have a cistern excavated at the lowest point of the natural hollow which was formed by the Cova da Iria, but it was not until November 1921 that it proved possible to carry out this request. One or two priests had different ideas as to where the well ought to be sunk, but it was José Alves who finally won them round, as Maria Carreira relates in this charming account:

"If you want my opinion," said José Alves, "you will never make a well here!" "Where, then?" asked one of the priests. "There" said José Alves, pointing to the place where the ground was lowest. "Even after a month or more without rain, that spot is always damp and there are a few rushes to be seen."

But after barely half a day's work, they met stone. "So what are you going to do now?" asked the priests. "Right now, we're going to blow the stone up!", he replied. No sooner had it been done than water appeared in abundance.

"Can it be said that the water appeared miraculously?" asked Father De Marchi. "That at least was the impression formed by the local inhabitants and the pilgrims, who flocked in ever-increasing numbers to the providential source." It is true that in this dry land, no one expected to find water so easily.

"People came with bottles and jugs", said the good José Alves, "and they filled them up, took them home, and gave the water to their sick to drink, or washed their wounds with it. Everybody had great confidence in this water, and to reward them, Our Lady took away their sufferings and healed their wounds. Never were so many miracles worked by Our Lady as at that time. Many came here with limbs which it was pitiful to see, running with pus. They washed themselves and left their bandages there because Our Lady had healed them. Others knelt down to drink this muddy water, and felt they had been healed of their internal ailments."

Father De Marchi commented: "It was as if the Most Holy Virgin, in her tenderness as a Mother, was making a game of men and the precepts of hygiene by accomplishing prodigies with matter which, humanly speaking, could only have been a cause of infection and further complications."

On 6 March 1922 the Capelinha was blown up by a dynamite explosion. However, providentially the statue of the Virgin had been taken out the evening before. There was general indignation throughout the country, but the outrage had one happy consequence. It was almost certainly this event which decided the bishop to commence the canonical process, which opened on 3 May 1922.

On 13 May 1922, the fifth anniversary of the first apparition, a crowd of some seventy thousand pilgrims — as many as had attended the great miracle of the sun — poured into the Cova da Iria, and Mass was celebrated in front of the Capelinha, which was still without its roof. At the last minute, the administrator of Vila Nova received a telegram from the government stating: "Reactionary assembly at Fatima absolutely forbidden". However this measure also back-fired on the government; the administrator advised the prefect that he would disobey the order, since it was quite impossible to carry it out.   The government was in fact compelled to withdraw its ban on the manifestation.

After the outrage of 6 March, the pilgrims poured into the Cova da Iria in greater numbers than ever. They were drawn thither neither by the seer, who had left Fatima one year before, nor by the beauty of the environment, nor by the clergy, who until now had done little or nothing to encourage them, nor by the chapel, which had been struck such a savage blow. Only the gentle presence of the Immaculate Virgin – invisible certainly, but almost tangible, and most efficacious – could draw almost irresistibly such a regular flow of pilgrims for each anniversary of the apparitions. Later, when he was congratulated on the magnificent success of Fatima, Mgr. da Silva could say, and it was the pure truth: "I have done nothing. It is the people and the Holy Virgin who did everything before I arrived."

On 13 October 1922 an edition of 3,000 copies of the first issue of a review was published, specially consecrated to the pilgrimage. With the authorisation of the bishop and under the direction of Canon Formigao, the *Voz da Fatima* was destined to make known throughout the whole of Portugal both the message of Fatima and the marvellous miracles of grace, the cures and the innumerable conversions which were being worked there by Our Lady of the Rosary. By 1925, the number printed had already risen to 50,000 copies; in 1929 it was 100,000; it continued to rise to 200,000 by 1934, and by 1937, twenty years after the apparition of Our Lady, 380,000 copies were being printed.

In 1923 and again in 1924 the authorities attempted to prevent access to the Cova da Iria, but in vain. In only a few years, the Virgin of Fatima had completely neutralised the storm of anti-clerical fury, which had been raging in the country almost without interruption for over a century and a half.

On 13 May 1924, the largest number of pilgrims ever

seen so far - 200,000 faithful - came to the feet of Our Lady. The Queen of Heaven graciously showed her pleasure, and, as had already happened on 13 September 1917 and 13 May 1918 the crowd watched as a rain of mysterious flower petals floated down from the sky and disappeared out of sight when they touched the ground. Mgr. da Silva himself attested to having seen this extraordinary phenomenon.

On 13 October 1924 the first stone was laid for the construction of the hospital for the sick. Thereafter, building was to continue unceasingly at the Cova da Iria, employing more than a hundred workmen for several decades. It is most remarkable that throughout all this time it was purely the spontaneous gifts of the faithful which sufficed to finance these works, and there was never any need to organise special appeals. This generosity of the Portuguese is a marvellous demonstration of their faith, their fervour and their filial recognition of their heavenly patron.

Cardinal Cerejeira has an excellent description of this first period of pilgrimage:

"In spite of the reserve of the Church and the obstinate and ridiculous opposition of the government, Fatima continued to stir the religious conscience of the country. Without the Church and contrary to the power of the State, the light of the miracle shone out with ever-increasing splendour in Portugal, and the warmth of the enthusiasm of the crowds of pilgrims made itself felt throughout the whole country". (Rome, 11 February 1967).

This movement of conversion was so profound that it was finally to make possible the political and social revival of the nation, which had been attempted so many times before, but always, until then, in vain. How was it, then, that this sudden, unhoped − for change had come about? Because from 1917, the powerful Virgin had promised to help her people, "if they obeyed her demands". Our Lady was keeping her word.

Chapter IV

PORTUGAL'S ASTONISHING
RENAISSANCE

"If you do what I tell you, many souls will be saved and there will be peace". Ten years had not yet elapsed after her promise, when, after converting a multitude of souls, the Virgin Mary was to give peace to her privileged nation, and this time in a manner which was to prove enduring, finally delivering Portugal from the yoke of revolution and religious persecution, at the very moment when its situation appeared more desperate than ever.

As we have seen, after the assassination of Sidonio Pais, while the Church had been able to preserve its liberty, the State had again relapsed into republican anarchy. An attempt to restore the monarchy in 1919, in the north of the country, failed. The financial situation was catastrophic, strikes increased, there was disorder everywhere. Between 1910 and 1926, there were no fewer than sixteen revolutions and more than forty new ministers.

On 28 May 1926, the army rose under General Gomes da Costa in the north, while General Carmona marched on Lisbon. The uprising corresponded so closely to the wishes of the whole nation that, in the words of the Portuguese historian, Father Oliveira Dias, "in three days it gained the whole country, and triumphed without having fired a single shot or spilt a single drop of blood – a fact which was absolutely unique in the history of military revolutions in Portugal. The faithful attributed this to a special protection of the Virgin of Sameiro", the great national shrine near Braga in the north, dedicated to the Immaculate Conception. (op.cit., p.630).

Power passed into the hands of General Carmona on 7 July, and on 25 March 1928 he was elected president of the Republic, an office which he retained until his death in 1951. However, the new government had still not been able to resolve the catastrophic financial situation which it had inherited, and so Carmona requested a loan from the League of Nations. This was granted, but on condition that the government would accept the permanent presence in Lisbon of one of its agents, to control the direction of the Portuguese economy. This was unacceptable, and so General Carmona was compelled to turn to the only man who seemed capable of saving the country from financial collapse.

Thus it was that, on 28 April 1928, Oliveira Salazar entered the government as Minister of Finance, thereby assuming the heaviest responsibility for the destiny of his country. Is it too much to talk of a political miracle, as well as a religious miracle? According to the historian Bainville, "of all the European states, Portugal is undoubtedly the one which had shown the signs of the most tenacious anarchy for the last thirty years" (Les Dictateurs, p.262).

It is a fact that, as from 1928, Portugal was to become the most politically stable country in all Europe. General Carmona remained president for a further twenty-three years, and Salazar was to remain head of government for forty years, until 1968! Whatever one may think, it is a fact that at that time, everyone – the vast majority of the Portuguese people, all the Portuguese bishops without exception, and Pope Pius XII himself – recognised that Salazar was the "man of Providence," granted by God to Portugal for the salvation of his country. That is a matter of recorded history, which can easily be confirmed by referring to the works of the best-informed historians of Fatima.

"A man of Providence"? Salazar was just that in the sense that he did not impose himself by demagoguery or political intrigues. No, he was called to power by the head of the State, because of his rare qualities – his unequalled skill in economics, his fundamental honesty, his evident disinterestedness – which made him indispensable to the national revival. However, while he was the only person capable of saving his country at such a critical hour, he was also and in the first place a devoted son of the Church. If he accepted power because he was called to it, he was also firmly resolved to implement, with prudence and tenacity, a social and political programme which was completely Catholic in inspiration.

Antonio de Oliveira Salazar came from very simple and poor peasant stock, from the village of Vimieiro to the north of Coimbra. He was hard-working, intelligent and pious, and in 1900 he entered the seminary of Viseu at the age of eleven. In 1905 he began to study theology, and was profoundly moved and influenced by Saint Thomas Aquinas. In June 1908 he received minor orders, but three months later he changed direction and decided not to become a priest. For the rest of his life, his faith was always lively and strong, never clouded by doubt, and his piety was discreet and free from all ostentation, but very deep. He remained faithful to the practice of daily Mass, and his life-long friend, Cardinal Cerejeira, said of him that he led the life of a monk.

In 1910 he entered the University of Coimbra, where he studied law and economic science. His success was so dazzling that he was given the chair of economic science before he had even received his degree. His friendship with Manuel Cerejeira, a young priest of his own age who was later to become the Cardinal Patriarch of Lisbon, dates from this period.

In 1921 he was elected to parliament, but the spirit of corruption so disgusted him that he returned to Coimbra the same evening, having only assisted at the first session. After the uprising in 1926, his reputation as an excellent economist resulted in the new government appealing for his assistance, but as they refused to

implement the strict control which he demanded over all
the State expenses, he returned to Coimbra after only a
few days, to resume his life as a professor.

When, two years later, he was pressed to accept the
office of Minister of Finance, far from accepting this
offer with enthusiasm, Salazar hesitated and postponed a
decision until the next morning. In the words of his
biographer:

"He wanted first of all to consult the opinion of his
friends. Cerejeira (the two friends were still sharing the
same flat), whom he was the first to consult, was openly
in favour of acceptance. Salazar was still hesitant; in his
great modesty he was afraid of such a rise to power. He
asked the opinion of a saintly priest, Father Mateo
Crawley-Boevey, the ardent apostle of the enthronement
of the Sacred Heart, who happened to be in Coimbra at
that time. Father Mateo was categorical; he strongly
urged Salazar that his duty obliged him to accept the
post. Salazar spent several hours that night praying
before the tabernacle, in a private chapel. Early in the
morning, Father Mateo celebrated Mass for his intention
and Salazar served it himself and made his communion.
Having made his thanksgiving, his indecision vanished,
and he stated: 'It is my duty to accept'" (Louis Mégevand,
Le Vrai Salazar, pp.72-73,190).

Salazar went to Lisbon, and as the government
accepted all his conditions, he entered office on 28 April
1928.

On his arrival, the budget was burdened with an
enormous deficit, the public debt was immense, and the
gold reserves were practically exhausted. Nevertheless,
by a veritable prodigy of science, prudence and courage,
within one year the new Minister succeeded in restoring a
disastrous financial situation. For the first time in a
quarter of a century, the budget which he produced for
1928-1929 was already able to show a surplus of several
million escudos. In a short time, the public debt was
eliminated, the gold reserves had been built up again,

and the escudo became one of the most stable monetary units in the world. The figures are given by Mégevand (op.cit,pp.74-80).

However, Salazar was not intoxicated by this success; his ideals were on a higher plane. On 4 July 1924, in a major speech to the Eucharistic Congress at Braga, he issued this noble definition of the Christian vision of the exercise of political power: "Not to seek for power as a right, but to accept and exercise it as a duty, considering the State as a ministry of God for the common good..." One day, not long after he had taken office, there was discussion in cabinet about a new proposal to impose a limitation on certain public observances of the Church. Salazar immediately recalled that he had accepted the ministry on condition that no limit at all would be put on the freedom which had been accorded to the Church, following the coup d'état of 26 May, and he forthwith handed in his resignation. That precipitated the resignation of the whole government, but Salazar was re-instated in the new government, and doubtless his stature had considerably increased in the estimation of General Carmona.

On 12 May 1929, Salazar went to Fatima accompanied by General Carmona and several members of the government. In the previous year, the wife and daughter of the president of the Republic had already assisted at the blessing of the first stone of the new basilica to be erected at the Cova da Iria. The occasion of the official visit this time was the inauguration of the new hospital, and it constituted the first official homage of the country's political leaders to Our Lady of Fatima. This official act of recognition by the authorities symbolized the marvellous transformation which had taken place in Portugal. In just a few years, the country had passed from being under the yoke of one of the worst anti-clerical regimes to a national government which was resolutely favourable to the Church.

In studying the origins of the cult of Fatima, a

notable fact which emerges is the extreme slowness with which the Portuguese clergy was moved to take an interest in it. Until 1920, Fatima depended in practice on the patriarch of Lisbon, Cardinal Mendes Belo, who was not favourably disposed towards the apparitions. Dr. Lisboa has recorded that later on his Eminence told him that he had come to admire Fatima, and that he did not want to die before being able to celebrate Mass at the altar of the basilica which was being built at the Cova da Iria. In fact he died in August 1929, aged 87, before he had had the opportunity to make public his acceptance of the cause of Fatima.

While it is true, as we have seen, that the bishop of Leiria had already taken the first indispensable measures for the development and good order of the pilgrimage between 1920 and 1926, it was only during the following years, from 1926 to 1931, that Fatima rose to the rank of a great national pilgrimage, enjoying the fervent and unanimous support of the whole hierarchy. If Our Lady was pleased to accompany her apparitions with innumerable prodigies, it was certainly with the object of attracting the mass of the faithful almost irresistibly to the Cova da Iria; but it was also, and much more so, to convince the authorities in the Church of the reality of her presence in this blessed spot, and of the truth of her message, and thus to lead the bishops and the Pope to honour her Immaculate Heart all the more, and to spread its cult throughout the whole Church. That is the essential point of her message. If the Virgin Mary is the all-powerful mediatrix, capable by herself of spreading throughout the world torrents of grace which would convert it completely, God wishes that She should grant them in response to the filial, public and solemn devotion of the shepherds of the flock towards her Immaculate Heart.

The example of Portugal is extremely significant: the extraordinary graces granted by Our Lady to the Portuguese people corresponded in an admirable way to the filial acts of devotion towards her carried out by the Portuguese bishops.

In August 1926, the Primate of Portugal, the Archbishop of Braga, and the Archbishop of Evora, visited the sanctuary incognito, and on the Feast of All Saints of the same year the Virgin of Fatima received an even more important visit. The apostolic nuncio, Mgr. Nicotra, was at Leiria for the commemoration of the seventh centenary of the death of St. Francis of Assisi. While at Leiria he expressed the desire to visit the monastery of Batalha, and Mgr. da Silva took him there. At Batalha, the representative of the Pope asked to be taken to Fatima and when he arrived at the Cova da Iria, he was profoundly moved by what he saw. Although it was not a pilgrimage day, there was a small crowd of people praying on their knees before the Capelinha, with a piety which is not seen anywhere else. The apostolic nuncio declared later, "it was as if Our Lady was present in the middle of these gallant people." At the end of the rosary, which was recited out loud by Mgr. da Silva, the nuncio, visibly moved, gave a short address to the faithful and granted them on the spot an indulgence of two hundred days.

On 13 December 1926, it was the Bishop of Madeira who led a pilgrimage to Fatima. The hierarchy was no longer simply granting permission for pilgrimages; by such gestures, which were to multiply rapidly from now onwards, the bishops were already showing their official recognition and giving a precious encouragement to the pilgrims. This in turn was to draw down on the land of Holy Mary an increase of graces and blessings from heaven. Following the people, the shepherds were responding in their turn with fervour to the message of the Immaculate Virgin.

On 21 January 1927, the Sacred Congregation of Rites granted to Fatima the privilege of being able to celebrate the Mass of Our Lady of the Rosary daily at the sanctuary. This concession was the first official act of the Holy See in favour of the pilgrimage.

But the event of the year was without doubt the inauguration, on 26 June, of the great Way of the Cross, which had been erected on the little mountain road from Batalha to Fatima. Beginning at the crossroads of Reguengo do Fetal, at thirteen kilometers from the sanctuary, the granite crosses are spaced out at one kilometer intervals. The procession, which set out at 8 o'clock in the morning, did not arrive until 2 o'clock in the afternoon at the Capelinha where, for the first time, Mgr. da Silva himself celebrated the holy Sacrifice of the Mass. Despite the ordeals of the route, four hundred pilgrims, who had kept the eucharistic fast since midnight, made their holy communion. With what zeal penance was practised in those days!

The first stone of the basilica was laid on 13 May 1928. A long report appeared in the *Osservatore Romano* on 3 June, from which the following brief extracts have been taken:

"The most solemn moment was the Mass of midday and the blessing of the sick. The Mass was celebrated by the Bishop of Leiria, and benediction was given by the Archbishop of Evora, in the presence of 300,000 faithful... When the statue of Our Lady was carried in procession from the chapel of the Apparitions up to the place where Mass was to be celebrated, in the presence of 400 sick people, 300,000 white handkerchiefs rose in the air to greet the Virgin, creating a marvellous spectacle... It looked as if an enormous flock of white doves was flying up to the sky... After benediction, the Archbishop of Evora addressed a vibrant appeal to the faithful, urging them never to fail to sing the glories of Mary, Patroness of Portugal, in Fatima and everywhere. 'Today was the greatest religious manifestation we have ever seen,' he added, 'and perhaps the greatest that has been seen anywhere.'"

On 1 October 1928, the apostolic nuncio visited Fatima for a second time, and during this year alone a million pilgrims visited the Cova da Iria. On 9 January 1929, at a reception for the Portuguese seminarians at Rome, Pope Pius XI offered them two images of Our Lady of Fatima, one for themselves, and the other for their families.

Another fact worthy of record took place at this time. The Dominican bishop of Portalegre did not want to admit the reality of the apparitions, and had even forbidden the public invocation of Our Lady of Fatima in his diocese. At a papal audience in 1929, he explained his reservations to the Holy Father. "How many seminarians did you have in 1917?" asked the Pope. "Eighteen, Holy Father." "How many do you have now?" "One hundred and twenty". "Then why are you waiting to go and thank Our Lady of Fatima?" It is interesting to note that on 25 March 1931, this bishop went to Fatima accompanied by all his seminarians, and he was the first bishop to celebrate pontifical High Mass at the sanctuary.

On 6 December of the same year, the Pope himself blessed a statue of the Virgin which had been presented by the sculptor, José Ferreira Thedim, to the new chapel of the Portuguese college at Rome, which had been dedicated to Our Lady of Fatima. Also at Rome, on 11 May 1930, not without the approval of the Pope, Father Gonzaga da Fonseca, S.J., gave an audio-visual conference on Fatima at the Biblical Institute, in front of a vast audience consisting of cardinals from the Curia, diplomats, professors and students of the Roman universities.

Although these simple gestures did not carry any official weight, they did at least manifest very clearly the thinking of the Holy Father at this period. When they became known in Portugal, they brought to the faithful and the apostles of Fatima the precious support of the blessing of the Sovereign Pontiff.

Finally, on 13 October 1930, thirteen years after the events in question, the bishop of Leiria, in his pastoral letter *A Divina Providentia,* pronounced his solemn judgement. Although this document was issued on his own authority, Mgr. da Silva later told Canon Barthas "that he had sent to His Holiness Pope Pius XI a complete dossier on the events of the Cova da Iria, and that after he had thoroughly studied it, the Holy Father had encouraged him to publish his approval..." (Letter of Canon Barthas to Father Alonso, 1 June 1967).

At the end of a long document which resumed all the proofs which had been supplied by the canonical enquiry, Mgr. da Silva concluded his pastoral letter in these words:

"...Humbly invoking the divine Holy Spirit and trusting in the protection of Mary Most Holy, after taking the opinion of the reverend consultors of our diocese, we adjudge right:

(1) To declare that the visions of the children at the Cova da Iria, in the parish of Fatima in our diocese, which took place from 13 May to 13 October 1917, are worthy of faith;

(2) To permit officially the cult Our Lady of Fatima".

These words are dry and cold in their canonical brevity, but they are also decisive and they filled with joy the one hundred thousand faithful who were present at the Cova da Iria on that 13 October 1930 – and all the more so because, doubtless, the faithful had also been informed of the new indulgences which the Holy Father had just granted to the pilgrims of Fatima, on the preceding 1 October.

Previously, the Holy Father had granted an indulgence of three hundred days for the invocation: "Our Lady of the Rosary of Fatima, pray for us". On 1 October, he granted:

(1) An indulgence of seven years and seven quarantines to each member of the faithful every time that he visits the sanctuary of Fatima and prays there, with contrition for his sins, for the intentions of the Sovereign Pontiff;

(2) A plenary indulgence once a month, on the usual conditions, to pilgrims coming in a group who pray for the intentions of the Sovereign Pontiff.

The solemn approbation of the apparitions, which had been awaited for so long, and the evident goodwill of the Sovereign Pontiff, aroused great enthusiasm throughout Portugal. Above all, it permitted the entire episcopate, united behind Cardinal Cerejeira, to manifest publicly its confident devotion towards the Virgin of Fatima.

Father Cerejeira, who had been professor of history at the University of Coimbra since 1919, had been appointed auxiliary bishop of Lisbon on 23 March 1928, and on 18 November he was chosen as patriarch in succession to Cardinal Mendés Belo. The young bishop, who was made a cardinal on 16 December 1929, quickly became the uncontested spiritual leader of the whole Portuguese episcopate. At first suspicious and reserved, he quickly became an ardent propagator of the cult of Our Lady of Fatima. He had become a spiritual son of Father Mateo Crawley-Boevey, on the occasion of the famous missionary's first visit to Portugal in 1927 - 1928, and had a deep devotion to the Sacred Heart and to the Immaculate Heart of Mary, to which he had consecrated his diocese on 1 June 1930.

Thereafter, each in his own sphere, and scrupulously observing the distinction of their respective offices – to the point of reducing their meetings to a minimum, the better to preserve their independence – the two friends of Coimbra University days, Salazar and Cerejeira, both of whom were called to the highest offices in 1928 and accepted them on the advice of Father Mateo, became the men who for the next forty years were to mould the religious and national rebirth of Portugal.

Accordingly it was decided to organise a great national pilgrimage of thanksgiving, to take place on 13 May 1931 under the direction of all the bishops of the country, who would then solemnly consecrate Portugal to the Immaculate Heart of Mary.

We know that this decision, on which, as we shall
see, was to depend the future of their country, was
taken by the bishops in the course of their retreat, which
was preached that year by Father Mateo, in the last days
of January 1931. On whose initiative was this act
proposed, which responded so precisely to the spirit of
the great Secret which had not yet been divulged at that
time? Father Alonso tells us, and this is important, that
it was Sister Lucia who inspired it. When and how did
she become aware that Heaven wanted her to ask all the
bishops of the country to consecrate Portugal solemnly to
the Immaculate Heart of Mary?

We do not know, and only the great work of Father
Alonso will doubtless provide the complete reply. How
did she communicate the divine will to the bishops? It is
not difficult to guess that it must have been through her
bishop, Mgr. da Silva, but he however, always
circumspect, proposed the national consecration to his
brethren without indicating from whom he had received
this noble idea.

Heaven never asks for anything impossible, and
divine Providence had prepared everything so well that
the majority of the bishops, if not all of them, were able
to accept this consecration to the Immaculate Heart of
Mary, without even knowing that it corresponded to a
formal request from Our Lady of Fatima. In fact, the
idea of a national consecration had already been widely
circulated and received with favour. In November 1928,
on the Feast of Christ the King, the Portuguese bishops
had already solemnly consecrated their country to the
Sacred Heart of Jesus, so the consecration to the
Immaculate Heart of Mary, which was proposed to them
in 1931, appeared as the natural consequence and
complement of this first act.

Once the decision had been taken Cardinal Cerejeira
drew up an eloquent appeal to the pilgrims, which was
published by *Voz da Fatima*, Issue No. 104, to which

the faithful responded with alacrity. Three hundred thousand people, some of whom had spent nine days on the roads, came to Fatima from all over Portugal, and in the presence of the apostolic nuncio and all the bishops of their country or their representatives, the patriarch of Lisbon pronounced the act of consecration in the name of them all.

After warmly thanking Our Lady for her apparitions at Fatima and for the shower of graces which she had continued to send down on the Cova da Iria, Cardinal Cerejeira said:

"The shepherds chosen by your Son to protect and feed in His name the flock whom He has acquired at the price of His Blood – in this 'land of Holy Mary', whose name cannot be pronounced without pronouncing yours – come here today as the official consecrated representatives of their flocks, in an act of filial homage of faith, love and trust, in order to solemnly consecrate the Portuguese nation to your Immaculate Heart. Take it from our fragile hands into yours, defend it and protect it as your very own; grant that Jesus may reign, conquer and govern in Portugal, outside Whom there is no salvation.

"We, the pontiffs of your people, can feel howling about us the fearful tempest which threatens to scatter and lead astray the faithful flock of those who bless you because you are the Mother of Jesus. In our affliction, we raise our hands in supplication towards your Son, crying out to Him: 'Lord, save us, we perish...'

"Intercede for Portugal, Our Lady, in this very grave hour, when furious winds blast us from the East, crying out for the death of your Son and the civilisation founded on His teaching, leading minds astray, corrupting hearts and kindling fires of hatred and revolution throughout the world. Help of Christians, pray for us!"

Here the Cardinal was referring to the recent events in Spain: the collapse of Primo de Rivera in January 1930,

the end of the Spanish monarchy and the exile of King
Alfonso XIII on 14 April 1931 (only one month prior to
the act of consecration which the Cardinal was at that
moment carrying out), the proclamation of the Republic
in Spain, the outrages on churches and convents, etc.
Only five years later, Catholic Spain was to be engulfed
by the horrors of the Communist – inspired civil war;
yes, Mary was indeed Portugal's last hope, its rampart
against a similar Communist insurrection.

And there were other dangers confronting them, as
the Cardinal made clear:

"Intercede for Portugal, Our Lady, in this troubled
hour when a foul wave of unbridled immorality, which
no longer even recognises the idea of sin, exalts the
demands of the flesh, even under the very Cross of your
Son, threatening to stifle the lily of virtue which is
nourished from the eucharistic Blood of Jesus. O
powerful Virgin, pray for us.

"Intercede for Portugal, Our Lady, in this hour of
passions and doubt when even the good run the risk of
being lost... Unite all Portuguese in obedience to your
Son, in love of the Church and also in the pursuit of
virtue, in respect for order and in fraternal charity.
Queen of Peace, pray for us.

"Finally, remember, O Patron of our country, that
Portugal formerly taught so many peoples to proclaim
you blessed among all women. In memory of what it did
for your glory, save it, O Virgin of Fatima, by giving it
Jesus, in Whom it will find Truth, Life and Peace."
(Obras Pastorais, vol. I, pp.289-292).

Although Portugal had already embarked on a sound
programme of recovery, the Cardinal nevertheless did
not hide his disquiet, for he knew how fragile was this
marvellous interior peace, he knew that it is a gift of
God, a grace from Our Lady, and that it is necessary to
merit it by continuous supplication.

This solemn act of consecration by the Portuguese
hierarchy, united with the fervent prayers and penance

of vast numbers of the faithful, brought down upon their country a new flood of graces. From then on, in response to this public act of devotion by the bishops to her Immaculate Heart, which corresponded so precisely to her wishes, the Virgin of Fatima was able to fully accomplish in full a veritable triple miracle, as we will see in the next chapter, in favour of the nation which was consecrated to her.

Appendix I

THE DIOCESAN PROCESS OF FATIMA

All the information and quotations which follow in these two appendices are taken from the long article by Father Alonso, entitled "Fatima, Proceso diocesano, Estudios y Textos criticos", published in *Ephemerides Mariologiae*, 1969, (pp.279-340).

Following the example of the Bishop of Tarbes in 1858, when investigating the apparitions of Our Lady at Lourdes, Mgr. da Silva published a "Provisao" on 3 May 1922, in which he nominated the members of the committee of enquiry.

It was headed by Canon Formigao, who was the first to enquire into and write the history of the apparitions, and seven other members, all of whom Father Alonso estimates to have been without any doubt the best possible people for the work. However, as one of the members of the committee himself remarked, it was unfortunate that Dr. Formigao was generally unable to be present except at the time of pilgrimages, which had the most regrettable effect of preventing any action being taken in his absence.

For example, there were the wonderful miracles of healing at Fatima which, at the time of the nomination of the commission in May 1922, were a patent and resounding fact. Canon Formigao has indeed collected them in his first book, but no attempt was made to carry out expert research in this field, and they did not even set up a sub-committee to study the whole question in conjunction with experts.

"Everything was left to the improvisation of the moment," says Father Alonso, "and it seems that over and above the apparitions, the Virgin Mary herself was expected to conduct the process!... Time passed, and witnesses slowly began to disappear... If the commission had set up a methodical system of work, facts and circumstances which are so difficult to re-establish later could have been uncovered very easily and we would have had a marvellous history of Fatima which could have been followed like a detailed chronicle of daily life. All these defects should not have existed in the process of the apparitions, which were so stupefying, so contemporary, so clear and evident, and with a multitude of witnesses who were so qualified by their presence, by their social position and by their psychological disinterestedness..."

However, despite its deficiencies, Father Alonso himself strongly affirms that the canonical process had access to amply sufficient material to enable it solemnly to affirm the authenticity of the apparitions with complete validity:

"The documents which it uses — and which should certainly have been infinitely more abundant in proofs, in witnesses and in interrogations — are nevertheless so numerous, and above all so important objectively, that they would lead the most rigorous historical criticism to the conclusion of a perfectly founded judgment..."

In fact, it is precisely because there was not the slightest serious opposition to the apparitions, and because the outstanding signs were so numerous and attested by all unanimously, that it was not thought necessary to prepare an exhaustive document on the events. Thus, regrettable though they may be, the very deficiencies in the canonical process indirectly testify to the incontestable truth of the apparitions.

Appendix II

THE MIRACULOUS CURES

As from 13 June 1917, at each of the apparitions Lucia transmitted to Our Lady numerous requests for cures. "I will cure some, but not others...", replied Our Lady. From this moment, She kept her promise, and with what liberality! A large number of extraordinary cures contributed to drawing the pilgrims to the Cova da Iria.

The first case on which Canon Formigao was able to conduct an enquiry was that of Maria do Carmo. A victim in the last stage of tuberculosis, she was declining every day. In July 1917, her doctor declared that she had only another fortnight to live. So she promised to go on foot to Fatima on the thirteenth of each month, four times in succession, to implore Our Lady for her cure. It was a distance of thirty-five kilometers from her village of Maceira, near Leiria, to the Cova da Iria. With heroic courage, she managed to get there on the thirteenth of August, and then again on the thirteenth of September, despite her extreme weakness, and she began to feel better. On the thirteenth of October, she made the journey again, in the pouring rain. At the moment of the apparition of Our Lady, she suddenly felt that she had been cured. If her cure was not as sudden as is demanded by the laws governing the discernment of miraculous cures, as set out by Pope Benedict XIV, it was nevertheless a perfect and definitive cure.

In 1923, in his work entitled *Os Acontecimentos de Fatima,* Canon Formigao cites some twenty-four cases of marvellous cures which had already taken place between 1917 and 1922. In 1927, all the third part of his great work *As Maravilhas de Fatima,* from pages 301 to 394, is consecrated to extraordinary cures. Finally, the pilgrim publication, *Voz da Fatima,* described more than 800 cases of cures which took place between the years 1922 to

1942. Some were so incontestable that Mgr. da Silva mentioned them in his pastoral letter authorising the cult of Our Lady of Fatima, as being among the miracles which prove the authenticity of the apparitions.

To take just one example, "the cure of Maria Augusta Dias, which took place on 4 February 1929, is particularly interesting because some of the greatest specialists in ophthalmology were concerned with her case, examined her, and drew up detailed medical certificates which leave absolutely no doubt at all about the cause and the evolution of her illness. The unanimous conclusion of these doctors was as follows: Maria Dias is incurable. Her optical nerves had wasted away, she could not see, and she would never be able to see again. However, after she had bathed her eyes three times in the water at Fatima a perfectly normal vision was instantly restored to her." (Agnellet, *Miracles à Fatima*, pp. 116 - 117).

Let us cite just one more absolutely amazing case, that of Margarida de Jesus Rebelo, who was cured on 13 May 1944. At the request of the Bishop Guarda, her cure was made the subject of a complete thesis by Dr. Mendes do Carmo, which was published in Lisbon the following year under the title, *Brilliant Miracle at Fatima*. Hers was a case of Pott's decease in a very advanced state, located on a fracture of the spine, and which had been diagnosed by X-rays. Her condition was complicated by a fistula or ulcer of the kidneys, which required permanent draining. Well! the patient, who was totally paralysed, was instantly cured at the moment of benediction of the Blessed Sacrament. At one stroke, all the symptoms of her disease disappeared, and she was able to get up, walk, and take food. "All her functions had been restored, and the ulcer, which only an hour before had been giving off a tuberculous pus, had disappeared and instantaneously closed up, leaving in its place completely new skin." (Agnellet, op. cit., p. 203).

Father Alonso reports that the saintly bishop of

Leiria, Mgr. da Silva, was not really in favour of an official medical bureau such as exists at Lourdes, to make the necessary scientific investigations and take depositions. He did not see the need for it. One day he said to Canon Barthas: "these good people go away from here cured by Our Lady; they do not ask for anything else, and nor does Our Lady. Why should they be troubled with these interrogations and enquiries, etc?" (Father Alonso, *Processo Diocesano*, p.334).

The three shepherd children, a few days before 13 October 1917. This photograph was published by Avelino de Almeida, to illustrate his articles of 15 and 29 October in *O Seculo* and *Ilustracao Portuguesa*.

The Virgin of Fatima showing her Immaculate Heart surrounded by thorns. This statue by José Ferreira Thedim was offered to the Carmel of Coimbra not after longer Sister Lucia was entered there, on Maunday Thursday, 1948.

Chapter V

PORTUGAL'S TRIPLE MIRACLE,
(1931-1946)

"There is only one word to describe what has happened here during these past twenty five years," said Cardinal Cerejeira on 13 May 1942, "and that is: miracle. Yes, we have the firm conviction that we owe the marvellous transformation of Portugal to the protection of the Most Holy Virgin."

This miracle of conversion is not something which historians have affirmed later, with the passage of time and the benefit of statistical analysis. No, it was so evident that it appeared as an incontestably divine marvel to the people who were living in those very times. Here we must quote the precious witness of Cardinal Cerejeira, who liked to recall how it was the sight of so many conversions which finally led him to believe in the apparitions of Fatima:

"I was one of those who, at the beginning, did not believe in the miracle. It seemed to me to be a poor imitation of Lourdes. At that time I was at Coimbra, not far from Fatima, a professor in the faculty of literature at the University, where I taught history. The event, which was the subject of passionate discussion at that time, was of absolutely no interest to me. Although the subject was hotly debated, I didn't even read the accounts in the papers.

"However, Fatima began to overcome both the prudent reserve of the Church and the violent opposition of the anti-clerical government of that time. The pilgrimage was continuously increasing. One heard of more and more amazing conversions, and even of cures... From my own house, huddled at the foot of the University, on the days of the twelfth and the thirteenth of the months of pilgrimage I could see the continuous files of cars, lasting for hours. This enthusiasm, which kept on growing from year to year, although deprived of any external support and even despite encountering some opposition, coupled with the knowledge of miraculous facts and the abundance of spiritual fruit, began to shake my indifference...

"In 1928, I was raised to the episcopate and made auxiliary to my predecessor, Cardinal Mendes Belo, Patriarch of Lisbon. There, I began to see for myself in the parishes the fervour which was aroused by the cult of Our Lady of Fatima. Some colleagues in the episcopate said to me: 'Go to Fatima, sit down in a confessional and you will see'. A Pentecost of conversions was truly manifest. I will never forget a former high school student, a ranting anti-clerical, who even used to go so far as to declaim in the streets, and who sought me out about this time to tell me that he had been converted at Fatima..." (Canon Barthas, *Fatima et les destins du monde*, pp. 7-8).

The Cardinal constantly used to repeat that it was this miracle of the conversions worked at the Cova da Iria which opened his eyes to Fatima. It would need a complete book in order to describe in sufficient detail the religious renovation which then took place in Portugal. We only have space here to give but one certain proof of it, that of priestly and religious vocations. As Pope John XXIII justly observed, this is the field which infallibly indicates the vitality of the Church.

The seminaries filled up at a prodigious rate. The figures are eloquent and need no further comment. In 1917, there were 18 seminarians in the diocese of Portalegre, but in 1929, when the bishop of the diocese visited Pope Pius XI, there were 120, and four years later in 1933 there were 201 ! When Mgr. da Silva arrived in the little diocese of Leiria in 1920, the seminary was closed; in 1933 it already had 75 seminarians. By 1933, in the Catholic bastion of the

North, there were 478 seminarians in the diocese of Braga alone!

As for priests, here are the figures for 1933 and for 1964, which show that the renewal begun by Fatima was no flash in the pan. In 1933, there were 2,618 priests in the province of Braga; by 1964, this number had risen to 3,188. The figures for the province of Lisbon rose from 950 in 1933 to 1,603 in 1964 and in Evora, which is in the South, and the most unchristian region of the country, the clergy nevertheless rose from 180 in 1933 to 277 in 1964. On average, during these thirty years, the number of priests increased by twenty-five per cent.

As for the religious, who had been expelled by the revolution of 1910, and forbidden by law until 1926, by 1934 there were still only 370 altogether throughout the whole country. By 1941, the Jesuits alone had risen to more than 300 out of a total of 1,321 religious who had been professed. In other words, the number of religious had almost multiplied by four in ten years!

The communities of nuns increased on the same scale. For example, the Dorothean Sisters, who received Lucia, only had one house left in all Portugal in 1917, at Asilo de Vilar, where they had been able to keep going by adopting civilian dress. By 1934, they possessed fifteen large houses of education or charity. By 1941, Portugal had some 3,815 professed nuns and their number continued to increase until recently.

There were also many other aspects to this great renewal of Christian life, such as the development of the Catholic press and radio, various pilgrimages and spiritual retreats, as well as a great lay movement of Catholic action, canonically erected by the bishops in 1934 under the title of "The pious union of the crusaders of Fatima", which quickly grew to more than 500,000 members! Firmly integrated into the main body of diocesan and parish life, this movement was consecrated by the bishops to the double cult of Christ the King and Our Lady of Fatima.

In order to arouse "this admirable and prodigious renewal of the religious life in souls", as Cardinal Cerejeira described it in 1942, in the collective pastoral letter for the jubilee of the apparitions, Our Lady of Fatima simply came to recall traditional Catholicism in all its vigour, that of the Gospels, and such as practised by Saint Louis de Montfort or Saint Maximilian Kolbe: The love of God and of the cross, a tender devotion to Mary, the rejection of Satan and of the world, self-renunciation, prayer and sacrifice. This is the religion which converted and transformed Portugal, to the point that in 1942 Cardinal Cerejeira was able to tell a French journalist: "You would hardly be able to find a handful of enemies of religion throughout the entire country".

Miracle is the word incessantly on the lips of the bishops on the occasion of the jubilee of the apparitions in 1942:

"If someone had shut his eyes twenty-five years ago and were to open them again today, he would no longer recognise Portugal, so profound and so vast is the transformation brought about by the factor of the modest and invisible apparition of the Holy Virgin at Fatima. Truly, Our Lady wants to save Portugal."

In order that the work of renewal should be more efficacious and lasting, the Virgin of Fatima was responsible for a radical change in the whole way of the nation's life, as Pope Pius XII did not hesitate to state himself:

"At a tragic moment of darkness and aberration, when the ship of State of Portugal, losing contact with its most glorious traditions and swept away by the anti-christian and anti-national tempest, appeared to be sailing straight towards a certain shipwreck... Heaven intervened in its goodness, and in the middle of the darkness the light shone out, order arose from the chaos, the tempest abated, calm was re-established, and Portugal was able to rediscover and renew the thread of its most glorious traditions as 'the Most Faithful Nation', in order to continue its glorious career as a people of crusaders and missionaries..."

"Honour to the worthy men, who were the instruments of Providence in such an undertaking".

This undertaking, which was led with such lucidity and courage by Salazar, was nothing less than a restoration based on authentic Catholic principles.

On 13 May 1931, fulfilling the demands of Heaven, the bishops of Portugal consecrated their country to the Immaculate Heart of Mary, so that She would save it from Communism, which at that time was gaining ground in Spain. However, it is not enough to say that it was She who accomplished this miracle of peace for Portugal.

If, as She stated in Her Secret (which was not to be made public until 1942), it is by Communist revolution that "Russia will spread its errors throughout the world, fomenting wars and persecutions of the Church", Our Lady showed in the example of Portugal that the most efficacious way to resist and overcome this peril is to raise up a state based on sound Catholic principles of social order.

Salazar's influence in the government had been growing since 1928, and on 5 July 1933 he became president of the cabinet. In 1936, on the tenth anniversary of the installation of the government, Salazar drew up a report on the work which had been accomplished so far, and which contains the following passages, showing his very clear perception of the problems faced by Portugal at that time:

"Russian Communism is in truth neither a political regime, nor an economic system: it is a doctrine, a religion. Through the intermediary of its apostles and its revolutionary agents, it claims to replace with its own ideas, throughout the entire world, the conceptions which the vast majority of civilised peoples have received more or less directly from the Catholic Church and from Christianity. But it is evident that very few people are aware that their respective principles are absolutely irreconcilable... Communism is the synthesis of all traditional forms of the revolt of matter against the spirit, and of barbarism against civilisation. It is the great heresy of our epoch...

"We are against all forms of internationalism, against Communism, against Socialism, against Syndicalism, against everything which diminishes, divides and dissolves the family, against class warfare, against the godless, against the purely materialistic conception of life, against force as the source of law. We are against all the great heresies of our times..." (*Comment on relêve un État*, Paris 1936, pp.17,21,29).

"To the souls torn by the doubt and negativism of this century, we have attempted to restore the consolation of the great certainties in life. Thus we have not questioned God and virtue; we have not questioned our country and its history; we have not questioned authority and its prestige; we have not questioned the family and its ethics; we have not questioned the glory of work and the duty of the worker". (op.cit,p.45).

Salazar was suspicious of an excessive and too hasty modernisation and industrialisation of life, and was opposed to the frantic materialism of modern life:

"At all costs we want to preserve from the wave which is sweeping over the world, simplicity of life, purity of morals, delicacy of feelings, the equilibrium of social relations, this modest but dignified family atmosphere which is the heart of Portuguese life" (Speech of 15 April 1937).

His ideal is that of Saint Paul, who calls for prayers "for kings, and for all that are in high stations, that we may lead a quiet and a peaceable life in all piety and chastity. For this is good and acceptable in the sight of God our Saviour." (I Tim.2:2,3). And is not this precisely the ideal of the great Pope Saint Pius X, who wanted to restore all things in Christ, and who wrote, in his Letter on the Sillon, "Civilisation is not waiting to be invented, nor is it a new city to be built in the clouds. It has been, and it is, the Christian civilisation, the Catholic city. All that remains to be done is to install it, and to restore it without ceasing on its natural and divine foundations."

Thus Salazar sought first of all to leave the Church complete freedom of action, and not to lessen its independence by making it depend on the State for material aid. In Portugal, the clergy were not supported by the State.

Moreover, Salazar chose to proceed very slowly, in order not to stir up the spirit of anti-clericalism, which had not yet died out in the towns. The decisively Catholic orientations of the new State were only introduced gradually, and thus it was only in 1940 that a Concordat was signed with the Holy See. This provided that "the Catholic religion and morality may be taught in all schools, to the pupils whose parents, or those who take their place, have not requested that they should be dispensed from this teaching." On the question of marriage, the State recognised all marriages celebrated according to the canon laws of the Church (Article 22), recognised the decision of the Church in cases of annulment (Article 25), and stipulated that, by the fact of their canonical marriage, both partners thereby renounced the legal option to ask for a divorce, which option, in consequence, was not available in the civil courts to the partners of Catholic marriages (Article 24). This sound measure greatly increased the number of canonical marriages, from some 70% in 1930 to 90% in 1960, and obviously the number of divorces diminished in proportion. In Braga, about 1960, there were only some 0.6% of civil marriages.

Many other examples could be quoted from the Concordat, showing how under Salazar the State brought help to the Church in her work for the salvation of souls. To take only one example, the "Missionary Agreement": nothing was overlooked in this document, to permit the maximum development of the Catholic missions in Portugal's overseas territories.

Thus it can be truly said that Salazar, in his position and according to the means available to him, helped Our Lady of Fatima to save Portugal. But, as we will see, Our Lady repaid him well, by helping him to overcome the tempests in which, without her benevolent protection and the support of the Church, he and all his work for the country would have been shipwrecked.

In his address to the Portuguese nation of 31 October 1942, Pope Pius XII mentioned "the red peril so close to you, so menacing, and which, however, had arisen so unexpectedly".

Since 1934, it was at the sanctuary of Our Lady of Fatima that the bishops of Portugal had reunited each year for ten days to make their spiritual exercises. When they met there in May 1936, events in Spain were progressing in an alarming manner. The elections of 16 February had proved a success for the Frente Popular and held the gravest forebodings for the future. What would be able to preserve their little country from this menacing wave of atheist and persecuting Communism which the Portuguese bishops contemplated arising in their neighbour? Lenin, it was well-known, considered it a matter of urgent priority to implant the Communist revolution in the Iberian peninsula. Thereafter, trapped between the two braziers of Russia and Spain, it would not be long before the whole of Europe would be in flames.

It was "with our hearts full of preoccupations and anxieties", as Cardinal Cerejeira was to write later, in the pastoral letter of the Portuguese hierarchy of Easter 1938, that on 13 May 1936 the bishops, at least all those of mainland Portugal, united in making a solemn vow which they kept secret for that year:

"They all promised to come on 13 May 1938 at the head of a national pilgrimage, to render solemn thanksgiving to the Most Holy Virgin, Mother of God, in the name of the whole nation, if She obtained for Portugal the victory over atheistic Communism and the blessing of peace...

"Before we separated", went on the Cardinal, "we placed our persons and our diocese more than once under the special protection of the Most Holy Virgin, victorious over all heresies and the protectress of Portugal." (*Obras Pastorais*, vol.2, pp.141-142).

As in 1931, the Portuguese bishops had preceded the event, for two months after they took their solemn vow, the assassination of the monarchist deputy, Calvo Sotelo, on 13 July 1936, marked the commencement of the Spanish Civil War. The great Secret of 13 July 1917 was beginning to be fulfilled to the letter: "Russia will spread its errors through the world, fomenting wars and persecutions of the Church. The good will be martyred..."

The menace was indeed grave for Portugal and, humanly speaking, it was almost inevitable that the nation should be infected by the revolutionary contagion. This is in fact what happened. On 8 September 1936, two warships mutinied and attempted to join the Red Brigades of Spain. However, Salazar reacted with firmness, and ordered them to be bombarded until they either surrendered or were sunk. This had the desired effect, and as a result the nation was preserved from the revolutionary virus. On 13 May of the following year, the bishops published a new pastoral letter, in which they vigorously denounced Communism and the horrors of the persecution which was then taking place in Spain, and at the same time informed the faithful of the vow which they had taken in secret the previous year.

However, by early 1938 General Franco was on the way to victory and all danger had finally been removed from Portugal, which had thus fortunately escaped the revolutionary contagion. When he announced the great national pilgrimage of 13 May, Cardinal Cerejeira solemnly gave thanks to Our Lady of Fatima for their preservation:

"Now that we have almost reached the moment for fulfilling our vow, we have every reason to rejoice in recognising that our confidence in the Patron of Portugal has not been in vain.   Since Our Lady of Fatima appeared in 1917... a special blessing of God has come down on the land of Portugal... Referring particularly to the period of the two years which have passed since we made our vow, we cannot fail to recognise that the invisible hand of God has protected Portugal, removing from our country the scourge of war and the leprosy of atheistic Communism.

"The blessing of peace, which the Church asks for so insistently in her liturgical prayers and which we asked for with confidence at Fatima, has been granted to us in an almost miraculous fashion." (*Obras Pastorais,* vol. 2, pp. 142-143).

500,000 pilgrims surrounded the twenty bishops of their country present at the Cova da Iria on 13 May 1938, and the national consecration to the Immaculate Heart of Mary was solemnly renewed, while millions of the faithful joined their prayers to this act in churches throughout the whole country. But while there was cause for rejoicing, there was also every need for continued supplication to the Queen of Heaven, for two months earlier Hitler had invaded Austria and well-informed people were aware of the tragic approach of a world conflict.   Would Portugal and Spain be able to preserve their neutrality? Such were the pressures of war that, humanly speaking, there was every reason to doubt it. But the supplication of the Portuguese nation to heaven was not to go unheeded.

On 6 February 1939, Sister Lucia wrote to her bishop, Mgr. da Silva, seven months before the declaration of war. At the same time as telling him that war was imminent, she also gave him a wonderful promise: in this horrible war, Portugal would be spared

on account of the national consecration to the
Immaculate Heart of Mary which had been carried out by
the bishops. Cardinal Cerejeira frequently repeated that
he had held in his hands this letter of Sister Lucia,
which had been sent on to him by Mgr. da Silva.

This is a little known point in the message of Fatima,
but of capital importance in the eyes of Sister Lucia,
who has frequently recalled it. For example, in a letter
dated 18 August 1940 to Father Goncalves, she wrote:

"The proof given to us by God (apropos the request
for the consecration of Russia in order to obtain its
conversion and thereafter peace in the world), **is the
special protection of the Immaculate Heart of Mary
over Portugal on account of the consecration which
has been carried out.** Those people of whom you tell
me have reason to be afraid (of the war). **All that
would have happened to us if our bishops had not
responded to the requests of our good God, and
earnestly implored His mercy and the protection of
the Immaculate Heart of Mary from the bottom of
their hearts."** (Father A.M.Martins, *Fatima
Documentos*, p.427).

Sister Lucia considered this remarkable prophecy of
peace for Portugal during World War II so important
within the whole context of the message of Fatima that
she decided to mention it in a letter which she wrote to
Pope Pius XII on 2 December 1940:

"Most Holy Father... Our Lord promises to give a
special protection to our country during this war, in
consideration of the consecration which the Reverend
Bishops of Portugal have made of the nation to the
Immaculate Heart of Mary. And this protection will be
the proof of the graces which God would give to the
other nations if, like Portugal, they were to consecrate
themselves to it" (ibid, pp.437-439). One could hardly
formulate a prophecy containing more precise details.
So, just what did happen? In the event, the prediction
was fulfilled to the letter.

In the latter half of 1940 Hitler put increasing pressure on Franco, and in an attempt to draw Spain into the war the Führer organised the famous meeting between the two leaders, which took place at Hendaya on the French-Spanish border, on 23 October 1940. He explained his plan to Franco: in order to conquer England, he had to take Gibraltar, to prevent British access to the Mediterranean and allow Germany to establish bases which would control North Africa. Accordingly, Hitler proposed an immediate alliance with Franco and the entry of Spain into the war in 1941.

With extraordinary skill, Franco succeeded in promising nothing. He certainly provoked the impatience of Hitler and the fury of Ribbentrop, but not to the point of attracting reprisals. Finally, on 7 December 1940, Hitler informed Franco that he had decided to attack Gibraltar on 10 January 1941, and he demanded free passage for his troops over Spanish soil. Portugal was not to be spared. Her harbours were to be occupied by the Germans, in order to give Hitler control over the Mediterranean and the Atlantic. The danger was so great that the Portuguese Government had made plans to transfer its seat to the Azores.

Once again, Franco had the courage to resist him. But what was there to have prevented the Führer from carrying on with his plans anyway, now that all his preparations had been made, and that the issue of the war depended on it? In human terms, not enough details are known to be able to answer this question clearly. But is it not interesting to note that at this very moment, when the future of the peninsular was in the balance, Heaven intervened again?

For on 8 December 1940, at the request of Sister Lucia, all the Portuguese bishops solemnly renewed the consecration of their country to the Immaculate Heart of Mary, in the cathedral of Lisbon, on the occasion of the feast of the Immaculate Conception, Patron of the kingdom.

After this refusal by Franco, curiously, Hitler hesitated. He thought that perhaps Mussolini would succeed in convincing the inflexible Spaniard, and so a meeting was arranged between the two leaders. But Franco promised nothing, and even succeeded in persuading the Duce to try and justify his own position to the Führer. Soon, Germany had to go to the aid of Mussolini in the Balkans, and then turn its attention to the Eastern Front. So it was that the greatest danger facing the two countries was finally lifted, and Portugal and Spain remained at peace throughout the rest of the war, without losing any of their territories.

On 13 May 1946, on the occasion of the great solemnities held to mark the third centenary of the consecration of Portugal to the Immaculate Conception, as well as the coronation of the statue of Our Lady of Fatima, Pope Pius XII explained to the Portuguese the supernatural meaning of the peace which they had enjoyed during the war:

"For four long years, the most terrible war which has ever ravaged the world prowled around your frontiers, but it never broke through them, owing above all to Our Lady who, from her throne of mercy, present like a sublime watchtower in the centre of the country, took care of you and of your governments; she did not allow the war to touch you, and you were only permitted a conjecture of the unheard-of calamities from which her protection preserved you."

Thus it is not being arbitrary to recognise in all this the work of a benevolent Providence and the accomplishment of the promise of Our Lady of Fatima. Her special protection for the country of Portugal which had been consecrated to her also extended to the Spain of Franco, purified by the blood of its innumerable martyrs in the Civil War; for, during the Second World War, Our Lady was also to communicate her requests and her promises through Sister Lucia to hasten the religious renaissance of Spain, and to preserve it from future chastisements, as we shall see in the next chapter.

It goes without saying that the Portuguese were fully aware of the immense grace and of the veritable miracle of peace which they had been granted. Let us hear once more the words of Cardinal Cerejeira:

"By a true miracle of love," he declared on 11 February 1942, speaking in the name of all the Portuguese bishops, "the Mother of God is keeping our country preserved and unscathed like a fragile vessel, miraculously safe in the midst of storms and apparently insurmountable dangers. Once again today we recall to you this debt of acknowledgment towards our glorious patron, because the peace which we enjoy — a true miracle which astonishes the world — is for us a witness and a pledge of her lofty patronage.

"Certainly, it would be unjust not to recognise the vigilant and patriotic action of our government... But there should not be a single Portuguese in good faith who does not recognise in our privileged situation, a reflection of that light which the Most Holy Virgin came to diffuse at Fatima... It is enough to contemplate this extraordinary state of affairs, in order to feel and recognise that a higher power has arisen and that a tender and merciful heart is lovingly watching over Portugal."

As for Salazar, far from attributing to himself any merit in preserving his country from the horrors of the war, he declared, on 7th May 1945:

"It was the will of Providence, in its high designs, that we were able to survive the conflict without being dragged into it directly and actively... Let us bless the victory! That is all I shall say about it. In this most solemn, not to say sacred hour, I only feel in myself a vivid outburst of gratitude towards the mercy of Providence, and pray that its light will illuminate the men responsible for the destiny of the world." (Discursos, vol. 4, pp. 95, 98).

Such then was the great design of God for our

century. He wanted the Immaculate Heart of Mary to convert the immense country of Russia, in the same way that it had marvellously converted the little country of Portugal. It is because the merciful designs of God cannot be undone by the slowness and resistance of men, and because His great design "to establish in the world devotion to the Immaculate Heart of Mary" is irrevocable, that the Portuguese miracle continues to be a pledge of hope for our time. In the words of Cardinal Cerejeira:

"Fatima speaks not only to Portugal but to the whole world. We believe that the apparitions at Fatima open a new era, that of the Immaculate Heart of Mary.

"What happened in Portugal proclaims the miracle. And it is the announcement of what the Immaculate Heart of Mary is preparing for the world" (*Obras Pastorais*, vol. 2, p.333).

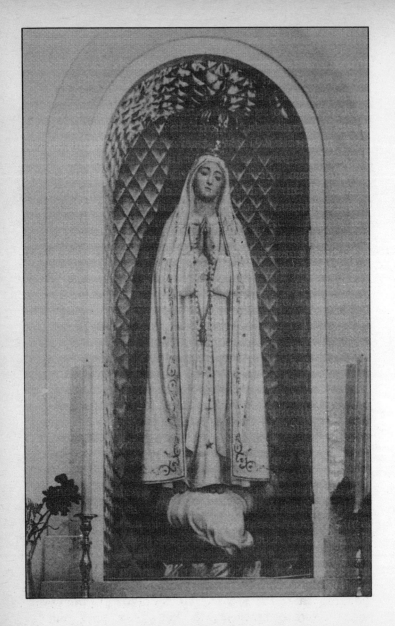

The first statue of Our Lady of Fatima, carved in wood by José Ferreira Thedim. It was blessed on 13 May 1920 and installed in the Capelhina, where it is still venerated today.

Chapter VI

SPAIN AND FATIMA, 1941 - 1947

In the Civil War from 1936 to 1939, and in the period of revolutionary unrest which led up to it, from 1931 to 1936, Spain had already suffered the terrible scourging foretold by Our Lady on 13 July 1917, "if people do not attend to my requests..."

But in 1941, the seer of Fatima received a new message from Heaven which directly concerned the state of the Church in Spain, the evils from which it was suffering, and the means which should be employed to remedy them.

Owing to the decisive work entitled *Fatima, Espana, Rusia,* which was published in Madrid by Father Alonso in 1976, as a resumé of his great critical work on Fatima, we are now able to throw a full light on this particularly unknown chapter in the history of Fatima. The author, who does not hide his very ardent love for his own Catholic Spain, very clearly demonstrates the importance of the messages from Heaven concerning his country. It also becomes clear, apart from its immediate application, that this grave warning has a much wider significance for the bishops of the Church.

Once again this divine communication took place on a Thursday evening during the holy hour which Lucia faithfully made each week, in conformity with the requests of the Sacred Heart at Paray-le-Monial. That particular Thursday also happened to be the feast of Corpus Christi, and moreover, that night doubtless Sister Lucia would be united in spirit with the pilgrims at the Cova da Iria who would be spending the night in prayer before commencing the ceremonies of 13 June. Here is the most complete account of this divine communication, which was sent by the seer to the

Archbishop of Valladolid, Mgr. Garcia y Garcia, the
former Bishop of Tuy, who was also one of her spiritual
advisers. Father Alonso cites the original Portuguese of
the text, which was written in January 1943, but
unfortunately he omitted a passage, which is indicated
by the dots between the brackets.

"In order to fulfil the wishes of our good God and of
your most reverend Excellency, I here set out, with the
greatest clarity that I can manage, the message which
the good God deigned to communicate to me in order to
be transmitted to you.

"With the permission of my superiors, it is my
custom to remain praying in the chapel up till midnight
on Thursdays. During these hours of very great
recollection, the good God is accustomed to
communicate so intensely with my poor soul that I do
not have any doubt at all about His real presence.
Ordinarily, after He has confounded me in my own
nothingness and my misery by making me feel what it is
about me that displeases Him, He continues by lamenting
this matter or that which causes Him such pain in the
poor world.

"**On 12 June 1941, He especially complained of
the coldness and relaxation of the clergy in Spain,
both regular and secular, and of the lukewarmness
and sinful life of the Christian people.** And He
continued thus: 'If the bishops of Spain were to meet
together each year to make their retreat in a house
especially chosen for that purpose, and if by common
agreement they decided what measures should be
followed to lead the souls which are in their care, they
would at that time receive special graces and lights from
the Holy Spirit.

'Make known to the Archbishop (of Valladolid) that I
ardently desire that the bishops should meet together in
retreat in order to agree a common policy between
themselves on the means to be employed in order to
reform the Christian people and to remedy the laxity of

the clergy and of large number of religious men and women. **The number of those who serve Me by practising sacrifice is very limited. I need souls and priests who serve Me by sacrificing themselves for Me and for souls (...).'**

"The good God will make your most reverend Excellency feel the reality of His desires and He promises to bless the effort which it will please you to make in order to satisfy them." (Father Alonso, *Fatima, Espana, Rusia,* pp. 64-66).

Here we are in direct line with the message of the Sacred Heart at Paray-le-Monial. In His great revelation of 16 June 1675, Our Lord complained about the infidelity of consecrated souls. The last sentences of this divine oracle are most frequently omitted, or else rendered less severe:

"Behold this Heart which has so loved men that it has spared nothing, even to exhausting itself and being consumed in order to show them its love. And for recognition I receive from the most part only ingratitude, by their irreverence and sacrileges, and by the coldness and scorn which they have for Me in this sacrament of love. But what is most painful of all to Me are the hearts who are consecrated to Me who treat Me like this. It is for this that I ask of you..." (Saint Margaret Mary, *Autobiography,* No. 92).

Curiously, the letter from which we have quoted, in which Sister Lucia relates in detail the divine communication which she received on 12 June 1941, was not written out until a year and a half after the event. The seer was to confess later on to having hesitated a very long time before making known this communication from Heaven to her directors. It is a fact that she experiences an extreme repugnance in having to reveal this sort of message concerning the disorders in the Church. There is perhaps another motive which might have encouraged her to keep silent about it. This message to Spain might have some connection with the themes of the Third Secret which Our Lord had not yet allowed her to reveal.

Whatever the reason, the months passed and Sister Lucia still continued to keep secret this complaint of Our Lord on the subject of the Church in Spain. At the end of November 1942, she received a long visit from Mgr. Garcia y Garcia, and not long afterwards she sent an account of it to her principal spiritual director, the Bishop of Gurza, in the course of which she said:

"Despite the great opportunity of this occasion to reveal Our Lord's wishes, timidity kept my mouth shut, and yet his most reverend Excellency asked me three times if I had anything else to tell him or to ask him, or if I wanted anything from him, etc. etc... Up till now, I have not spoken of this desire of Our Lord, for fear that I am ordered to reveal it." (Father Alonso, op. cit., p.60).

This in fact is what happened. The Bishop of Gurza immediately wrote back to her, assuring her that this communication certainly came from God and that it must be transmitted without any further delay to the Archbishop of Valladolid.

In response to further encouragement from the Bishop of Gurza, and perhaps also to answer certain of his questions, on 28 February 1943 Sister Lucia wrote a long letter which is quoted in its entirety in the latest book of the Jesuit authority on Fatima, Father A.M.Martins. In it she describes with precision the various divine communications which she had already received previously, but she also alludes at the same time to new divine locutions, which she had received during a holy hour on a Thursday night for which she does not give the exact date.

"The good God has already shown me His contentment with the act carried out by the Holy Father and by several bishops, although not complete according to His wishes. In return, He promises to put an end to the war soon. The conversion of Russia is not for now.

"If the bishops of Spain take note of the wishes of Our Lord and undertake a true reform of the people and of the clergy, well and good! If not, (Russia) will again be the enemy by which God will give them a further chastisement.

"The good God will allow Himself to be appeased, but He complains bitterly and sorrowfully about the very limited number of souls in a state of grace who are willing to renounce themselves according to what the observance of His law demands of them.

"Here is the penance for which the good God is asking today: It is the sacrifice which each one ought to impose on himself in order to lead a life of justice in the observance of His law. And He wishes that this way should be clearly explained and made known to souls, because many interpret the word penance in the sense of great austerities, and as they have neither the strength nor the generosity to undertake them, they become discouraged and fall back into a life of tepidity and sin.

"Finding myself in the chapel with the permission of my superiors on Thursday night, at midnight Our Lord said to me: 'The sacrifice which is required of everyone in accomplishing his own duties and the observance of My law, that is the penance for which I ask and which I now require.'

"And as for myself, your most reverend Excellency, I ought to be the first to submit myself in everything to the orders and the wishes of the good God. And for that, in order to obey what you told me in your last letter, I send you this declaration. The good God does not make these manifestations to me by means of apparitions, but by giving me an intimate and intense feeling of His presence in my soul." (Father A.M.Martins, *Fatima e o Coracao de Maria*, pp.104-105).

Let us note in passing that, without in the slightest way seeking for it on her part, Sister Lucia has had the privilege of being directed and advised during the course of her life as a seer by an impressive series of priests whose intelligence, supernatural wisdom, spirit of discernment, and even often their personal holiness were unanimously recognised. Doubtless this corresponded to a design of Providence, for all of them were thus able to guarantee the authenticity of her apparitions or divine communications... Not one of these eminent ecclesiastics who have had the privilege of knowing the secrets of her soul has ever doubted any more than did Mgr. da Silva or Cardinal Cerejeira, the authenticity of the divine communications she was receiving.

Owing to the zeal of the Bishop of Gurza, for whom this letter was destined, this message was soon to cause a great stir, first of all in Portugal and then in Spain. It was read out publicly on two occasions very favourable to its divulgation. The first occasion was on 20 April 1943, at Fatima, at a retreat based on the exercises of Saint Ignatius which was being preached to a group of doctors, lawyers, engineers and other leading members of Portuguese society. During the month of May, it was also read to the Portuguese bishops who had met at the Cova da Iria for their annual retreat. For Spain, a copy of the letter had been sent to the Archbishop of Valladolid.

Is not this solemn warning on the real penance which Our Lord wants more relevant than ever today? Heaven is not asking the faithful to spend hours in prayer or practise impossible austerities, which would only serve to inflate self-love, before causing souls to fall back into a life of tepidity and sin, in discouragement and despair. No! The way which is proposed at Fatima is much more humble and more sure. Let us at least make every effort to please God by renouncing sin and by fulfilling the duties of our state in life as best we can. This was the golden rule of Pope Saint Pius X, who used to say "do your duty and all will go well!"

The universality of Our Lord's requirement is also

inescapable: "The penance for which I am asking and which I now require, is the sacrifice which is required of each person in accomplishing his own duty and the observance of My law." Everyone without exception in the whole Church is specified — the simple faithful, but also priests and religious, bishops, cardinals and even the Holy Father. This history of Fatima is a holy history which God is directing sovereignly as a most good and most merciful Father, and it is precisely because of His jealous love and His infinite mercy that He also acts with justice and severity. Peace or war, the happy or unhappy destinies of our countries and of the world, finally depend on the zeal with which the Christians — and first of all, that of their leaders, the Pope and the cardinals, and of their bishops, priests and consecrated souls — correspond with faith and docility to the holy wishes and great designs of His Heart.

Sister Lucia's letter of 27 May to the Bishop of Gurza throws further interesting light on this subject:

"I am very pleased at the news you have given me of the consecration (of a parish or a community to the Immaculate Heart of Mary) because it reveals much love for the Immaculate Heart of our heavenly Mother, who is so good, and also, through her, for our good God. They love us so much! And Their most ardent wish is to see that Their love is known, and that people correspond to it. It is one of Their usual complaints: 'I love and I am not loved; I make Myself known and I am not known; I give and no response is made (to My advances)...'

"They love and desire this cult (of the Immaculate Heart of Mary) because They use it to draw souls to Themselves, and that is all They desire: *to save souls, many souls, all souls; salvar almas, muitas almas, todas almas* (emphasised by Sister Lucia). A few days ago Our Lord said to me; **'I most ardently desire the propagation of the cult and devotion to the Immaculate Heart of Mary, because this Heart is the**

magnet which draws souls to Me, it is the furnace
which casts over the world the rays of My light and
of My love, it is the inexhaustible source from
which gushes forth over the world the living waters
of My mercy.'

"If these communications are certain (and that is how
I feel them to be despite so many fears), I do not want to
prevent them from being communicated to souls. That
is why I give them to you. They are not mine, I am
nothing. Do with them whatever you consider most
useful for the glory of God." (Father A.M. Martins,
S.J., *Fatima e o Coracao de Maria*, pp.62-63).

And so, as we have seen, the message to the Church
of Spain is accompanied by a terrible threat: if the
bishops take account of the wishes of Our Lord and
undertake a true spiritual reform, all will be well! But if
not, Russia will again be the enemy by which God will
once more give them another scourging. It could hardly
have been made more clear that the terrible Civil War
was a divine chastisement for the Church of Spain,
which had become gravely unfaithful to its holy
traditions.

Let the people of Spain at least draw the lesson from
this terrible trial of purification. Such is the meaning of
the message of 12 June 1941.

This warning to Spain might at first appear rather
severe, coming only four years after the heroic crusade
during which thirteen bishops, more than seven
thousand priests and religious men and women, as well
as several hundred thousand of the faithful, had given
their blood for the Catholic faith. Had not a marvellous
effort at Catholic restoration begun immediately after the
victory in April 1939? The fact is beyond doubt, and we
cannot do better than to quote the enthusiastic words
addressed by Pope Pius XII to the new ambassador of
Spain on 17 December 1942, precisely at the moment
when Sister Lucia had decided to inform the Archibishop
of Valladolid of the severe warning from Heaven:

"As for us, looking at you as a Father, and supporting you with our prayers, and, at the opportune moment by our words and encouragements, we have followed day by day a really splendid recovery which raises so many hopes in us for the welfare of Spain. We have admired the continual manifestations of public or private piety and faith (...). We have heard you say that your 'way of life would not be perfect if it was not profoundly Catholic', and that 'you uphold a hundred times over the most absolute orthodoxy'. For the great consolation of our soul we have heard of the progress of Catholic Action, and of the abundance of good and solid priestly vocations; we have seen Christ triumphant in the schools; we have seen churches rebuilt on their smoking ruins and the Christian spirit penetrate into the laws, the institutions and all the manifestations of official life. Finally, we have contemplated God present once again in your history..." (*Documents Pontificaux de S.S. Pie X*, 1942, pp. 321-323).

In other words, just as in Portugal, as we have seen, the harmonious co-operation between Church and State was already yielding much good fruit in Spain. But Our Lord had likewise complained in almost identical terms about Portugal in a communication to His messenger in 1940, which she expressed in these words in a letter to Cardinal Cerejeira on 19 December 1940:

"Our Lord is displeased and afflicted on account of the sins of the world and those of Portugal. He complains at the lack of conformity with His wishes, at the blameworthy life of the people and, in particular, at the tepidity, the indifference and the too easy life led by the majority of priests and religious men and women. The number of souls who serve Him in prayer and sacrifice is very limited."

What hard words! And yet, let it be said, the blameworthy life of the people and the laxity of the clergy and of consecrated souls surely cannot have been as bad in these two countries, where an undeniable

Christian renaissance was taking place, as in other nations. On the contrary. But Our Lord, who had preserved them, as if by a miracle, from the terrible chastisement of the war which was raging throughout the whole world at that time, had the greatest designs of mercy upon them. These two nations, whom the Queen of Heaven had chosen for her manifestations in our century, were without doubt the first to be called to put into operation the requests of the message of Our Lady. Thus they were to become, for other peoples, a dazzling window through which could be glimpsed the incomparable blessings granted to them through the mediation of the Immaculate Heart of Mary.

That is why these divine reprimands, and even these threats, far from being a sign of any reprobation, were much rather the mark of a real predilection. They call to mind the words of Saint Paul:

"You have forgotton the consolation, which speaketh to you, as unto children, saying: My son, neglect not the discipline of the Lord; neither be thou wearied whilst thou art rebuked by him. For whom the Lord loveth, he chastiseth; and he scourgeth every son whom he receiveth.

"Persevere under discipline. God dealeth with you as with his sons; for what son is there, whom the father doth not correct? But if you be without chastisement, whereof all are made partakers, then are you bastards, and not sons." (Heb. 12:5-8).

The bishops of Portugal, as we have shown, took very seriously this message from Heaven transmitted by the seer of Fatima. On 2 February 1941 they published a collective pastoral letter on the "anxieties of the war and the necessity for expiation", which was plainly inspired by the message transmitted by Sister Lucia. Lengthy extracts are quoted in Father Martins' work, *Fatima, Caminho da Paz,* (pp. 82-85). Father Alonso adds that "at this period, Sister Lucia was responsible for numerous initiatives taken by the Portuguese hierarchy, which produced the best and most beneficial results for the Christian people" (op.cit., p.74).

As we will see, the Spanish bishops eventually followed this example and, as if by a miracle, their country was saved from the terrible threat of Communism in the years 1945-1946. But at first they were slow to respond.

In anticipation of the unfavourable reaction of certain of his brethren in the hierarchy, the Archbishop of Valladolid decided to wait before transmitting to them the message which he had received. Meanwhile, he questioned Sister Lucia again: "Could this not be the fruit of some illusion?" With her usual humility, the seer replied that she herself had had her doubts, but that "her spiritual director had assured her that it came from God". The Archbishop was convinced, and he wrote to Lucia:

"That is well, my daughter. I can tell you the following for your peace of mind: There is here, in Spain, a soul to whom Our Lord also makes communications, and He has revealed exactly the same thing to this person. Now you must beseech Our Lord to help me to overcome the difficulties which are numerous, above all on the part of the government." (Father Alonso, op.cit.,p.72).

In the event, Spain was spared, and we follow Father Alonso, who lived through the events of those times, in not hesitating to recognise in that fact a further example of the miraculous protection of the Virgin of Fatima. In the conclusion of his work *Fatima, Espana, Rusia,* from which the quotations above have been taken, the Spanish expert wrote:

"...It is the Virgin who removed from Spain the Communist scourge which was threatening it 'for the second time'. In reality, at the end of the Second World War, when the shameful agreements of Yalta and Potsdam had delivered us inexorably into the hands of Russia, this scourge hung over us again, like a fateful sword of Damocles. The leaders of the West were working in a suicidal fashion - as has happened so many times in the subsequent years - by demanding of Spain a process of democratization which was certain to lead to sovietisation. **But God, through the intercession of the Virgin of Fatima, delivered us from this infamous chastisement.**" (op.cit.,p.139).

The Spanish bishops firmly resisted to a man the international chorus directed against Franco, and we know the reason why: it is because they had received with the greatest respect the solemn warning from Heaven, which had been transmitted to them by Sister Lucia some years before. They had undertaken the "true reform of the people and the clergy" which Our Lord required of them, and, divinely forewarned of the terrible scourge which threatened them anew, they understood the gravity of events and were able to react with prudence, for the good of the Church and the peace of their country.

Chapter VII

THE EXAMPLE OF THE KING OF FRANCE

Earlier, in a divine communication very similar to those related in the preceding chapter, Sister Lucia recounted how Our Lord dictated specific prayers He wanted her to say to His Mother for the conversion of Europe and the entire world, and then complained to her about the delay on the part of the Church in fulfilling His will. This communication took place in the little maritime town of Rianjo, near Pontevedra, where she had been sent in August 1931, to rest and recover her health.

Let us quote first of all from the letter of 29 August 1931, in which the seer transmits to her bishop this very important revelation:

"My confessor orders me to impart to your Excellency what took place, a short time ago, between our good God and myself. As I was asking God for the conversion of Russia, Spain and Portugal, it seemed to me that His Divine Majesty said to me: **'You console Me greatly by asking Me for the conversion of these poor nations. Ask it also of My Mother, and say to her often:**

'Sweet Heart of Mary, be the salvation of Russia, of Spain and Portugal, of Europe and of the entire world. And on other occasions say to her: By your pure and Immaculate Conception, O Mary, obtain for me the conversion of Russia, Spain, Portugal, Europe and the entire world.'

'Make known to My ministers, that as they follow the example of the King of France in delaying the execution of My wishes, they will follow him into misfortune. It will never be too

late to have recourse to Jesus and Mary.' " (Father Alonso, *Fatima Ante la Esfinge,* p.97).

Three years later, Sister Lucia was to make explicit mention of this memorable letter which she wrote from Rianjo:

"As for Russia," she wrote to Father Goncalves on 21 January 1935, "it seems to me that you will greatly please Our Lord by working so that the Holy Father will carry out His designs. About three years ago (therefore, around 1931), Our Lord was distinctly displeased because His will was not being carried out. I made this known to the bishop in a letter."

In 1936, when she drew up for Father Goncalves the detailed account of the apparition of Tuy, she decided to include in the same text the decisive relevation of August 1931:

"Later, by means of an intimate communication, Our Lord complained to me: **'They have not wanted to listen to My request !... Like the King of France, they will repent of it, and they will do it, but it will be late. Russia will have already spread her errors throughout the world, provoking wars and persecutions against the Church. The Holy Father will have much to suffer.' "**

To whom is Our Lord referring in this terrible prophecy? To Sister Lucia's confessors? Her Bishop? Or the Holy Father? The historians of Fatima do not tackle the question and Father Alonso himself leaves us in uncertainty. However, the words of Our Lord in August 1931 are sufficiently explicit by themselves, and they unquestionably indicate that it is a question of the realisation of the message and not of its transmission, which had already been done. "Like the King of France..." In 1689, King Louis XIV was required to **execute** the wishes of the Sacred Heart, not to **transmit** them, which was the duty of the Reverend Father de la Chaise. Our Lord's words at Rianjo clearly refer to the same people ("My Ministers") who "have not wanted", who "will repent of it" and who "will do it" in the end. Thus His words can only refer to the Pope and to the bishops on whom it is incumbent to fulfil the consecration requested by Our Lord. It is probable also that by the use of the plural, the prophecy also concerns the successors of the reigning pontiff, in the same way that the requests of the Sacred Heart were addressed, in the person of Louis XIV, to all his heirs on the throne of France.

It is in fact this explicit reference to the demands of the Sacred Heart, addressed to Saint Margaret Mary in 1689, which gives us the full significance of the brief words of Our Lord's instruction to Sister Lucia for the pontiffs of our century, some three hundred years later: "Make known to My ministers, considering that they follow the example of the King of France in delaying the execution of My demands, that they will follow him into misfortune." Once again the message of Paray-le-Monial throws a bright light on that of Fatima, while at the same time this revelation finally clears up the thorny historical question of the transmission of the message of the Sacred Heart to King Louis XIV. For certain historians, arguing from the absence of any contemporary document attesting that the King had been properly notified, thought quite simply that he had never known about it. The words of Our Lord to Sister Lucia have definitely settled the debate. The King did finally become aware of Our Lord's wishes, but "he did not want to listen to them" and "he delayed their execution".

On 17 June 1689, on the feast of the Sacred Heart, which was already celebrated in the monastery of the Visitation of Paray-le-Monial, Saint Margaret Mary spoke to the Reverend Mother de Saumaise, with regard to King Louis XIV. After she had described what the Sacred Heart was expecting of the Visitation monastery, the Saint continued:

"...but He does not want to stop there. He has even

greater designs which can only be carried out by His omnipotence, which can do whatever it wants.

"He desires, it seems to me, to enter into the mansions of princes and kings with pomp and magnificence, to be honoured there to the same extent that He was outraged, despised and humiliated in His Passion, and He wishes to receive as much pleasure in seeing the great of the earth abased and humbled before Him, as He felt bitterness at seeing Himself prostrated at their feet.

"And here are the words which I heard on this subject: 'Make known to the eldest son of my Sacred Heart' – speaking of our King – 'that as his temporal birth was obtained by devotion to the merits of My holy Infancy, in the same way he will obtain his birth in grace and eternal glory by the consecration which he will make of himself to My adorable Heart, which wishes to triumph over him and, acting through him, over the leaders of the world.' He wishes to reign in his palace, to be painted on his standards and engraved on his arms, in order to render them victorious over his enemies, beating down at his feet their own vainglorious and arrogant leaders, in order to render him triumphant over all the enemies of the holy Church" (Letter 100, *Vie et oeuvres de Sainte Marguerite-Marie Alacoque*, vol.2, pp.437-438, Gigord 1920).

In another letter, written on 28 August of the same year, the messenger of the Sacred Heart again detailed the wishes of Heaven and the incomparable promises which were attached to them:

"The eternal Father, wishing to repair the bitterness and anguish which the adorable Heart of His divine Son suffered in the mansions of the princes of the world, amidst the humiliations and outrages of His Passion, wishes to establish His empire in the court of our great monarch, whom He wants to use to carry out this design, which He wishes to be accomplished in the following way, namely: To put up a structure on which would be displayed a painting of this Divine Heart, for It to receive the consecration and the homage of the King and of the whole court. Furthermore, this Divine Heart wishes to become the protector and defender of his sacred person against all his enemies visible and invisible, and to assure his salvation by this means. That is why He has chosen him as His faithful friend, that through him the Mass in His honour should be authorised by the Holy and Apostolic See, obtaining from it all the other privileges which should accompany this devotion to the Sacred Heart.

"By this means He also wishes to grant him the treasures of His graces of sanctification and salvation, by distributing an abundance of His blessings over all his enterprises, which He will cause to succeed for His glory by giving good fortune to his arms, so that he will be triumphant over the malice of his enemies. How happy he will be if he develops a taste for this devotion, which will establish for him a reign of eternal honour and glory in this Sacred Heart of Our Lord. Jesus Christ will take care to raise him up, and to make him as great in heaven before God His Father, as this great monarch will take it upon himself to relieve Our Lord in the sight of men of the disgrace and frustration which this Divine Heart has suffered at their hands. This will come to pass when the King renders Him the honours, love and glory which He awaits from him.

"But as God has chosen the Reverend Father de la Chaise for the execution of this design, by the power which He has given him over the heart of our great King, it will be up to him to make the matter succeed..." (Letter 107 to Mother de Saumaise, op.cit.,pp.456-457). The Sacred Heart added that as the Jesuits had been specially chosen to spread the devotion towards Him and to transmit His great designs to the King, the Order would in return receive graces and blessings if it fulfilled this responsibility, but that it would be punished if, on the contrary, it did not do so.

Well ! The prophecy was fulfilled to the letter, and in a striking fashion. It is practically certain that Father de la Chaise refused to transmit the message of the Sacred Heart to the King, or that in any case he did not encourage him to comply with it. A terrible chastisement followed: within scarcely a century the Jesuits, who were the most flourishing and powerful Order at that time, fell into ruin. Suppressed in Portugal in 1759, in France in 1764, and in Spain three years later, the Society of Jesus was finally dissolved by the Pope himself in 1773. Saint Alphonsus Liguori commented: "What can one do but adore in silence the judgments of God and keep our souls in tranquillity..." (Father T. Rey-Mermet, *Le Saint du Siécle des Lumiéres*, 1982, p.573).

As for King Louis XIV, who learnt about the wishes of the Sacred Heart from a source other than the Jesuits, the year 1689 marked a turning-point in his reign. Despite all his genius, his incessant labours, and his heroic patience in the face of the worst reverses, he did not succeed in crushing his enemies in a decisive manner: Calvinist Holland, and Protestant England and Prussia.

The great King died piously in 1715, but isolated and already powerless to avert the catastrophes which were threatening Catholic France. His kingdom, deprived of the extraordinary graces and miraculous help which had been promised to him by the Sacred Heart, was gravely menaced abroad and undermined from within by cowardice, laxity and fatal errors, which were soon to bring about its downfall. Throughout the eighteenth century, the 'philosophes' and the encyclopaedists were striving with all their power against God and His Church and the monarchy, to bring about the great upheaval of the French Revolution.

So it came about that on 17 June 1789, **exactly one century later to the very day** after that feast of the Sacred Heart, when Saint Margaret Mary, "following the motion which was given to her at that instant", had drawn up for the King the great designs of Heaven, the rebellious Third Estate proclaimed itself the Constituent Assembly. From that moment the legitimate power of the monarchy was overthrown, and barely four years later, on 21 January 1793, France, ungrateful to and rebellious against its God and its Catholic monarchy, put to death its King on the scaffold.

The parallel between the revelation to Saint Margaret Mary at Paray-le-Monial in 1689 and that to Sister Lucia in August 1931 is all the more striking as Our Lord Himself explicitly referred to Paray-le-Monial in the latter revelation. The meaning of Our Lord's words to Sister Lucia is clear beyond doubt, and the consequences, if His Will is not complied with, will be terrible: by their lack of docility to the voice of Heaven, the Sovereign Pontiffs today, like the King of France three centuries ago, will bring down misfortune upon themselves, and upon the Church and all Christendom, under attack from the enemy upon all sides.

Cardinal Cerejeira, patriarch of Lisbon

Chapter VIII

THE CHURCH EMBRACES FATIMA,
1942-1946

"The Virgin Mary has taken a position of extraordinary prominence in the Catholic Church of today, culminating in the Marian years at the end of the pontificate of Pope Pius XII: the definition of the dogma of the Assumption in 1950, the centenary of the dogma of the Immaculate Conception in 1954, and the centenary of Lourdes in 1958." These facts, as stated by Abbé Laurentin, in his book *La Question Mariale* (p.15), are incontestable, but what the author does not tell us is that this incomparable surge of devotion towards the Holy Virgin took root and developed in close connection with the Message of Fatima, especially from 1942 to 1948.

In fact, although the majority of the historians of the reign of Pius XII either pass over the event in silence, or only give it a derisory mention in the history of his pontificate, it was the consecration of the Church and of the world to the Immaculate Heart of Mary, on 31 October 1942, which was at the origin of this great movement of Marian devotion. This movement continued to increase from year to year until almost the end of the pontificate, accompanied by an equally marvellous expansion of the Catholic faith.

Let us recall very briefly the most notable events which marked the twenty-fifth jubilee year of Fatima in 1942.

8-13 April: Marian Congress at Lisbon with the first 'route of Our Lady', whose statue was carried in triumph from the Cova da Iria to the capital of the Portuguese empire.

18 April: Cardinal Schuster divulges the major themes of the great Secret.

April to May: Publication at Rome of the works of Fathers da Fonseca and Moresco, which at one stroke were to make the message of Fatima known throughout the whole world. Both these works were published with the imprimatur of the Vicar-General of the Vatican City, and by authorising these two works to be printed at the Vatican polyglott press, the Sovereign Pontiff thereby conferred upon them a particular authority and indirectly guaranteed the authenticity of the facts which they reported. That was a sign of approval of great importance for the authors and their works, because up to that time none of the previous books published on Fatima had mentioned the new themes which they were now revealing. Tens of thousands of copies of these new books on Fatima were printed in a matter of months, and thus served to spread throughout the whole world the message of Our Lady and the devotion to the Immaculate Heart of Mary.

13 May: At Fatima, impressive ceremonies for the twenty-fifth anniversary of the first apparition, and at Rome, Pope Pius XII celebrated the twenty-fifth jubilee of his episcopal consecration.

13 October: The blessing of the massive crown of gold offered by the women of Portugal to our Lady of Fatima. Eight kilogrammes of gold had been collected, but the dimensions of the statue were such that it was only possible to utilise 1,200 grammes of gold; the crown also contained 2,650 precious stones of various kinds and 313 pearls. The crown was blessed at the Capelinha by the Cardinal Patriarch, and after the Mass the Cardinal read out a formula of consecration of Portugal to the Immaculate Heart of Mary. On the same day, those families who had not been able to get to Fatima were invited to make their consecration to the Holy Family, in memory of the apparition of the Infant Jesus and of Saint Joseph to the little seers on 13 October

1917. Ceremonies of devotion also took place in many of the towns, of which the most beautiful was that in the new parish church at Lisbon dedicated to Our Lady of Fatima. There was a magnificent torch-light procession in the evening in the streets.

But the most important event in this year of 1942 was the publication throughout Portugal on 13 October of the third edition of *Jacinta*. In this work, Father Galamba quoted the essential passages from the third and fourth Memoirs of Sister Lucia, and made known to the public the exact and complete text of the Secret of 13 July, exactly as the seer had written it down in 1941.

We can hardly over-estimate the importance of this publication which, for the first time, unveiled to the Portuguese public all the most specific and important themes of Fatima, in their harmonious unity: the vision of hell, Russia, wars and persecutions, and the Immaculate Heart of Mary. Moreover, the work contained a remarkable preface by Cardinal Cerejeira and a prologue by Mgr. da Silva, who thus gave it practically the authority of an official publication of the Portuguese episcopate. The Cardinal even ended his address at the High Mass at the Cova da Iria by reading some extracts from his preface to *Jacinta*. Here is his beautiful conclusion:

"The miracle which this charming book describes to us is the interior miracle which took place in the souls of the happy children to whom it was given to see the 'Mother of Fair Love'... If it was not being too daring, I would go so far as to say that it is Our Lady who has written this book in the souls of the seers. Did not Saint Paul say that the Christians were 'a letter of Christ written, not with ink, but by the Spirit of the living God'? Paraphrasing him, one could thus say that *Jacinta* is a letter of the Most Holy Virgin destined to be read by souls. It tells us, more clearly than words, what Our Lady came to do at Fatima, and what She wants from us.

"The mystery begins to clear up. Already Fatima is speaking not just to Portugal, but to the entire world. We believe that the apparitions of Fatima have opened a new era, that of the Immaculate Heart of Mary. What took place in Portugal proclaims the miracle. It is the announcement of what the Immaculate Heart of Mary is preparing for the world." (op.cit.,pp.5-6, 8th edition 1982).

31 October: Closure of the Fatima jubilee. Radio message from Pope Pius XII to the Portuguese nation and consecration of the Church and of the world to the Immaculate Heart of Mary. In the mind of Pius XII, this act, which was a first official response to the request of Fatima, was intended to direct and inspire the devotion of the whole Church in the future, and thereafter he took care to recall it and to underline its importance.

In order to indicate its relationship with Fatima, the Pope had decided to carry out this consecration to the Immaculate Heart of Mary on the occasion of the closure of the jubilee of the apparitions in 1917. But as it had been pronounced in Portuguese, it was likely to pass almost unnoticed in the rest of the world, so Pius XII decided to renew it again without delay in order to give it a much wider impact. On 8 December 1942, on the feast of the Immaculate Conception, "a ceremony of expiation and of supplication" took place in the basilica of Saint Peter's. In the presence of forty cardinals, numerous bishops, the diplomatic corps, the clergy of Rome and a great crowd of pilgrims, the Holy Father read out again the formula of consecration of the world to the Immaculate Heart of Mary.

Responding to the most formal revelation of the divine will at Fatima — "God wishes to establish in the world devotion to my Immaculate Heart" - he earnestly invited the whole Christian people to unite themselves with the act of devotion to the Virgin Mary which he had just carried out: Bishops by consecrating their dioceses to her, the clergy their parishes, and the faithful by consecrating themselves.

With exemplary zeal, in the last days of 1942 numerous parishes in Italy consecrated themselves to the Immaculate Heart of Mary and, still before the end of the year, a number of dioceses in France and Spain also followed this example. Among the religious orders, the Franciscans, Capuchins and the Servites likewise made the consecration.

1942 had also seen the first public decision of the Sovereign Pontiff in view of the proclamation of the dogma of the Assumption of the Most Holy Virgin. In order to make clear the wishes of the Church, Pius XII gave to two Jesuits the task of drawing up and publishing all the petitions relative to the Assumption of the Virgin which had been addressed to the Holy See during the past century.

In the same year, another important decision was taken for the increase of devotion to the Virgin. On 11 January 1942, Pius XII signed the decree "De Miraculis" re-opening the cause of canonisation of Saint Louis - Marie Grignion de Montfort.

All these various acts served to point the Church towards a more perfect response to the requests of the Virgin of Fatima. The fact is remarkable: from 1942 until 1948, each year was notable for several decisive events in the development of devotion to the Immaculate Heart of Mary.

On 15 April, once again the Pope prescribed public prayers to the Most Holy Virgin to obtain peace, recalling at the same time the solemn act which he had carried out a few months earlier:

"In the month of October last, we vowed, confided and consecrated to the Immaculate Heart of the Blessed Virgin the holy Church, the mystical body of Jesus Christ, torn by so many wounds, and at the same time the entire universe which, consumed by hatred and embittered by divisions, expiates the punishments due to its own iniquities. We learnt with very great consolation for our paternal heart that this act of devotion was renewed almost everywhere by the bishops, priests and the multitude of the Christian people. But if almost all Christians have consecrated themselves spontaneously and voluntarily to the Immaculate Heart of the Virgin Mary, they must also voluntarily and resolutely conform themselves to her, if they really wish the Mother of God to receive their prayers with goodness" *(Documents pontificaux*, 1943, p.95).

In Rome, the subject of Fatima had aroused the greatest interest. Five editions of Father da Fonseca's book were published in 1943 alone, and on 12 February he gave a conference on Fatima at the Vatican. In March, Father Luigi Moresco spoke on Fatima in the great hall of the Gregorian University, and so many people came that he had to give the same talk again on two further occasions.

At the same time, Pius XII multiplied the acts by which he made clear his personal devotion. In March 1943, he himself blessed a reproduction of Our Lady of Fatima for the Church of Saint James of Udino. In June, he accepted the official request of Portugal to be allowed to construct at its own expense a chapel dedicated to Our Lady of Fatima in the new church of Saint Eugenio, which had been built in Rome to commemorate his episcopal jubilee. Portugal gave all the marble for this chapel.

On 29 June, in his encyclical *Mystici Corporis Christi,* the epilogue of which was entirely devoted to "the Virgin Mary, Mother of the members of Christ", the Pope ended by once again recalling the act of consecration to her Immaculate Heart. Finally, on 25 November he prescribed that the 8 December following, which was the first anniversary of the act of consecration in the basilica of Saint Peter's, public prayers should again be addressed to the Virgin Mary, accompanied by works of penance carried out in a spirit of expiation.

Throughout the whole year, the movement of consecrations to the Immaculate Heart of Mary had continued to increase. In Spain, for example, not only dioceses, but also parishes and all sorts of religious, civil or military associations had carried out this act of devotion towards the Virgin. Father Alonso lists forty-one Spanish dioceses which made their consecration to the Immaculate Heart of Mary in 1943, usually after the publication of a pastoral letter in which the bishop explained the meaning of the act and its close relation with the message of Fatima.

In France also, the consecration carried out by Pius XII was to bring forth marvellous fruits of grace. It was to inspire "the Great Return", "this extraordinary mystical event, without doubt the greatest act of homage rendered to the Mother of God on our land of France", in the words of Father Devineau, who was first of all one of its principal organisers, and then its enthusiastic historian.

It all began in 1938, on the occasion of the tricentenary of the consecration of France to Our Lady by King Louis XIII. At that time four reproductions of the statue of Our Lady of Boulogne, seated on her ship, had visited several hundred parishes in the north of France. Four years later, on 7 September, one of them was received at Lourdes with honour. Shortly after 8 December 1942, Cardinal Suhard, Archbishop of Paris, made his visit *ad limina*. Pius XII must surely have told him about the consecration to the Immaculate Heart of Mary which he had just carried out. On his return, the assembly of the cardinals and archbishops of France fixed the Sunday of 28 March 1943 for the consecration of all the dioceses of France to the Immaculate Heart of Mary.

"This consecration," wrote Father Devineau, "was the charter of the Great Return. When on 28 March 1943, the Church of France, by the mouth of its spiritual leaders, made its own this act of the Pope, Our Lady of Boulogne – who from then on was to be called Our Lady

of the Great Return – left Lourdes for the first stage of
her progress over the roads of France. The prodigious
circuit had begun. It was to last for sixty months, and
to spread throughout numerous countries of Europe and
from there to the rest of the world." (Father L.
Devineau, O.M.I: *Une extraordinaire odyssée dans le
sillage de la Vierge*, pp.13-18).

In five years, this Marian mission of a new type,
entirely centred on the consecration to the Immaculate
Heart of Mary, was to visit more than 16,000 parishes in
83 dioceses in France. The programme was simple:

"By day, it was long marches on foot from one parish
to another, often drawing immense processions,
whatever the weather, in summer just as in winter, in
sunshine, frost, snow... The night was spent in the
pulpit and the confessional. A few hours of sleep and
the next day it moved on. It was another Lourdes every
day in several parishes in France; grace was poured out
in floods" (op.cit.,pp.27-28).

On the road, they sang and prayed for hours on end,
and many walked bare foot. Everywhere, the pilgrim
Virgin was greeted by crowds "with a fervour and faith
which it is difficult to imagine today. Twenty years
later," wrote Father Devineau in 1963, "it is difficult to
realise just how far the whole people were uplifted by
enthusiasm and fervour... Under the fragile appearance
of the statues which passed by was hidden the presence of
the Mother of God. It was She who was the great
convertor of souls, the great missionary" (op.cit.,p.35).

"From 26 April to 4 July 1943" wrote Mgr. Theas,
"the statue of Our Lady of Boulogne travelled the length
and breadth of the small diocese of Montauban... The
confessionals and the altar rails were besieged during
these holy nights, while the churches resounded to the
multitudes reciting the mysteries of the Rosary. In
certain parishes there were spectacular conversions such
as had not taken place on missions". (op.cit.,pp.35-
36).

In the course of her letter to Pope Pius XII on 2 December 1940, Sister Lucia wrote:

"And now, Most Holy Father, allow me to make one more request. It is only an ardent desire of my poor heart, that the feast in honour of the Immaculate Heart of Mary should be extended to the whole world as one of the principal feasts of the holy Church".

On 4 May 1944, this wish was partly granted. On that day the Pope instituted the feast of the Immaculate Heart of Mary in order, as he specified, to preserve the memory of the consecration of the human race to this same heart, which had been carried out by him on 8 December 1942.

"God wishes to establish in the world devotion to my Immaculate Heart". The institution of this feast marked a new step forward in the realisation of God's designs of mercy for our century.

It was also in 1944 that the message which Sister Lucia had received from heaven on 12 June 1941 was finally transmitted to numerous bishops of Spain. The first initiatives directed towards the Spanish hierarchy by Mgr. Garcia y Garcia in 1943 had been rather poorly received, especially by the cardinals of Toledo and Seville. In the face of this set-back, Mgr. da. Silva decided to act, and on 10 February 1944 he sent the following letter to each of the bishops of Spain:

"I am the unworthy Bishop of the smallest diocese in Portugal, but the diocese which was chosen by Our Lady for the apparitions of Fatima. Sister Lucia, one of the seers, is still living in a religious house in Spain. I have spoken with her and I have often corresponded with her. Not long ago, she wrote to his Excellency, the Bishop of Gurza, who is also the superior of the society of Portuguese Catholic Missions, and her former spiritual director, and she sent him a letter whose contents I hereby communicate to you. Father Moran, S.J., who has come to Fatima several times to preach the spiritual exercises presided over by his Eminence Cardinal

Cerejeira, Patriarch of Lisbon, has insisted that I should make known to your Excellencies these words of Sister Lucia."

This intervention very rapidly produced the happiest results. The Bishop of Badajoz, who was the first to reply to this circular letter, said to Mgr. da Silva:

"The words of Our Lord to Sister Lucia of Fatima could not be more expressive, and they voice with perfect exactitude what is taking place among us. In consequence, as far as my weak forces permit, I will attempt to follow the warning of Our Lord in order to appease His justice, which is offended by so many souls who live without fulfilling His holy law."

Cardinal Segura, Archbishop of Seville, changed his mind:

"What truths are contained in these affirmations! We see it happening every day and we repeat it constantly to our faithful. May the Lord, by the mediation of Our Lady of Fatima, for whom Spain has such a tender devotion, grant us the change of morals which is indispensable for the realisation of His divine designs on our people!... I sincerely thank Father Moran for his intervention on this subject, I have known him since my childhood and I have a high opinion of his virtues and his good qualities, his gifts, his knowledge and his prudence."

From then on the Cardinal was so convinced of the supernatural origin of the message transmitted by Lucia that he went so far as to read it out publicly in his cathedral, in one of the Lenten conferences for which he was celebrated throughout the whole of Spain.

The text of this letter was also published in the Spanish-English edition of the *Voz da Fatima,* and then reproduced in numerous popular reviews. **A few bishops found it slightly irritating, but the majority received this severe warning with the greatest respect**. If the opposition of some prevented the episcopal reunions which Our Lord had requested, His message was widely diffused and, as a whole, the bishops strove to comply with it. Indeed, when in 1947 to 1948 the Virgin of the Cova da Iria began her missionary travels throughout the world, her greatest triumph was reserved for Catholic Spain, and it was there also that she was to pour out with the greatest liberality her marvels of grace and her miracles of healing and conversion.

On 2 March 1945, Sister Lucia wrote to Father Aparicio: "I am delighted at the progress which devotion to the Immaculate Heart of Mary is making in all directions. In the state of the world today, it is this devotion which will save us." As for the Pope, he did not lose any occasion to invite the Christian people to advance in this direction.

On 21 January, he addressed the Marian congregations of Rome on their role and on what is the nature of true consecration to Mary. On 8 April he again referred to the Immaculate Heart of Mary, and on 15 April he published the encyclical *Communium interpretes*. In the latter, he prescribed public prayers to the Virgin to obtain peace, and again insisted on the necessary reform of people's public and private morals which should accompany such acts of devotion, thereby adopting the warning of Our Lord to the bishops of Spain:

"Since it is the sins which we commit in front of God (Baruch 6,1) which turn us away from Him and precipitate us into misfortune and ruin, it is not sufficient, as you well know, venerable brethren, to send up ardent prayers to heaven; it is not sufficient to come in very great numbers to the altar of the Blessed Virgin Mary, bringing offerings, flowers and supplications; but it is also absolutely necesssary to renew the public and private life of the people by the adoption of Christian morals..."

On 8 December he gave an allocution for the closure of the spiritual exercises in the Vatican, in the course of which he stated:

"If, at times, we feel ourselves bending under the weight of the cross, if the lack of understanding or the injustices of the world fill our heart with bitterness, if the attacks of the enemies of God submit our courage and our perseverance to a hard trial, we know, on this day consecrated to the Immaculate Virgin, where we may find consolation and security: in our devotion to Mary, the heavenly Queen, Mother of God and our Mother. Trusting in her intercession, we will make our way forward securely under the divine protection."

After the jubilee celebrations of 1942, devotion to the Most Holy Virgin reached a new height in the year 1946, and especially devotion to the Virgin of Fatima

On 1 May 1946, the Pope confidentially sent to all the bishops of the world a copy of the encyclical, *Deiparae Virginis*, and asked them individually to give him their opinion on the definition of the dogma of the Assumption of the Most Holy Virgin and whether they considered it was an opportune time for its promulgation.

On 30 June, addressing the faithful of Belgium, he evoked "the Immaculate Heart of Mary, Mother and mediatrix". On 16 July, he broadcast a magnificent radio message to the faithful of Columbia, on the occasion of their national Marian Congress, explaining that it was their intense devotion to the Virgin Mary which preserved the faith of the people "in the countries colonised by mother Spain". As Our Lady of Mount Carmel was to be crowned in the course of the Congress, the Pope concluded by referring to a theme which is the very essence of the message of Fatima: that it is the Virgin Mary, and she alone, who will gain the decisive victory over the forces of evil that have been unleashed:

"...From our position as pilot of the barque of Peter, when we hear the tempest howling and see the sea rising up in fury as if to overwhelm our ship, we serenely and confidently raise our eyes to the Virgin of Mount Carmel

– Respice stellam, voca Mariam – and we beseech her not to abandon us. And, although hell does not cease to assail us and the fury of the forces of evil increases daily, counting on her powerful protection we will never doubt that the victory will be ours."

On 31 July the Pope wrote a letter on the rosary to the Archbishop of Manila for the Marian Congress in the Philippines, and on 30 August and 4 September he again alluded to the Immaculate Heart of Mary. On 22 November he gave an address to a group of leaders of the Great Return in which he encouraged them to continue their work:

"Keep on with your work, and keep to the road which you have chosen: That is the right one. It is the road of prayer and penance, the royal road of the cross... The most difficult thing is not experiencing the fervour of all-night vigils, or processions made barefoot under the burning sun or the frost, if these are only momentary episodes. The most difficult thing is constant fidelity to one's duties as a Christian, even when they are troublesome, to pious practices, and to the little sacrifices of daily life in a spirit of reparation, humility and love.

"We can only recall here what we said on this subject on an anniversary most dear to our heart: 'Consecration to the Mother of God... is a total gift of oneself, for all one's life and for eternity; by no means a gift of pure form or sentiment, but an effective gift which should be realised in the intensity of Christian and Marian life.' (Address of 21 January 1945 to the Congregations of the Holy Virgin)."

1946 was also the year when Poland made the act of consecration to the Immaculate Heart of Mary. But it was also, and above all, the great year of the triumph of Our Lady of Fatima in Portugal.

We have already recounted how, for the jubilee of the apparitions, the women of Portugal had offered to the Virgin of Fatima a massive crown of gold, enriched with pearls and precious stones, which Cardinal Cerejeira had solemnly blessed on 13 October 1942. But the ceremony of the crowning of the statue of Our Lady had been reserved for better days.

As the third centenary of the consecration of Portugal to the Immaculate Virgin was approaching, the bishops of the country decided to solemnise this national anniversary by carrying out the coronation of the statue of Our Lady of Fatima, so they turned to the Pope and asked him to send a pontifical legate for the ceremony. When this favour was granted, on 18 January they issued a collective pastoral letter announcing the programme of festivals in honour of the tercentenary, and inviting all the people of Portugal to take part in the great national pilgrimage of 13 May.

On the evening of 10 May, before boarding the aeroplane which had been put at his disposition by the Portuguese government, Cardinal Aloisi Masella, legate *a latere,* went to ask for a last blessing from the Holy Father. "Reflect on the greatness of the mission which you are going to fulfil", Pope Pius XII told him; "you are going to crown Our Lady Queen of the world."

Despite the wind and the rain, some 800,000 pilgrims had assembled to greet their Queen with indescribable enthusiasm. At the crowning, the president of the League of Catholic Women presented the golden crown, in the name of the women of Portugal who had offered it, to the Minister of the Interior, the delegate of General Carmona, Head of State; the Minister in turn handed it to the legate who, in the name of the Sovereign Pontiff, placed it on the forehead of the venerated image. Father da Fonseca, who was a professor at the Biblical Institute at Rome, and who witnessed the ceremonies as a member of the suite of the Cardinal legate, has left us this account of what happened next:

"The feelings of the crowd gave way to an irrepressible outburst of applause, vivas, hosannas,

prayers, and tears of love, devotion and enthusiasm...
Only those who were there at such an exceptional
moment in the history of Portugal and of the world can
have any idea of what it was like. The consecration of
Portugal to the Immaculate Heart of Mary was renewed.
Then the hymns, the hosannas and the invocations to
their Queen and Patron broke out again... But soon, at
exactly half past eleven, a profound silence spread
throughout the vast arena and the voice of the Pope
began to ring out." *(Nossa Senhora da Fatima,* p.205).

"Venerable brethren and dear sons...

"When, four years ago, in the midst of the din of the
most deadly war there has ever been in history, we found
ourselves for the first time in your midst, rising up in
spirit to this holy mountain, in order to thank Our Lady
of Fatima with you for the immense blessings with which
she had recently gratified you, to the Magnificat of all
hearts we joined a cry of filial confidence, that the
Immaculate Queen and Patron of Portugal would
complete the work which she had so marvellously begun.

"Your presence today in this sanctuary, in a
multitude so immense that no one can count it, testifies
that the sovereign Virgin, the Immaculate Queen whose
maternal and compassionate Heart brought about the
prodigy of Fatima, has granted your supplications in a
super-abundant manner. An ardent and grateful love
has led you here, and you have sought to give it a
sensible expression, symbolising it by this precious
crown, the fruit of so much generosity and sacrifice, and
which, by the hand of our Cardinal legate, we have just
placed on the miracle-working image of Our Lady of
Fatima.

"If, in the eyes of the heavenly Queen, this expressive
symbol is a witness to your filial love and your gratitude,
it reminds you first of all of the immense love manifested
by the countless blessings which the Virgin Mother has
spread throughout the 'land of Holy Mary'.

"Eight centuries of blessings ! The first five passed

under the sign of Our Lady of Alcobaca, Our Lady of Victory, and Our Lady of Belem, during the epic struggles against the Crescent for the foundation of the nation... The last three centuries have passed under the special protection of the Immaculate. The monarch who restored the independence of Portugal, proclaimed her Patron of his kingdoms and domains with the whole nation united in the Cortes, and consecrated his crown to her as a tribute of his vassalage, taking a vow to defend to the death the privilege of her Immaculate Conception.

"And the most faithful Virgin has not disappointed the hope which had been placed in her. It is sufficient to consider the last last three decades which have passed, and which, in terms of the crises traversed and the blessings received, are equal to centuries. It is enough just to open one's eyes and to see this Cova da Iria, which has been transformed into a gushing source of grace, of physical prodigies, and much more of miracles of the moral order which pour out in torrents all over Portugal, and, thence crossing her frontiers, extend over all the Church and the entire world.

"How can one not give thanks? Or rather, how can one give thanks worthily?

"Three hundred years ago, the monarch of the national restoration, as a sign of the love and gratitude of himself and of his people, laid his royal crown at the feet of the Immaculate, the Queen and Patron of his kingdom. Today, it is all you, the whole people of the 'Land of Holy Mary', with the shepherds of your souls and your government who – to your ardent prayers, your generous sacrifices, your eucharistic solemnities, and the thousand forms of homage which your filial and grateful love has inspired – have joined in offering this precious crown to encircle the forehead of Our Lady of Fatima. You have united here in this blessed oasis, impregnated with the supernatural, where her marvellous protection is felt in the most tangible manner, and where you all feel more near to her

Immaculate Heart, which beats with an immense tenderness and a maternal solicitude for you and for the entire world.

"How precious is this crown ! What an expressive symbol of love and gratitude !"

In moving words, the Holy Father then described how the spectacle of this immense concourse of the faithful at Fatima in honour of their Queen evoked in his mind the sublime spectacle of the entrance of the glorious Virgin into heaven.

"...And the Empyrean saw that She was really worthy to receive honour and glory and empire; because She was more full of grace, more holy, more beautiful, more divinized, incomparably more so than the greatest of the saints or the most sublime of the angels, taken separately or altogether; because She was mysteriously related, in the order of the hypostatic union, with the whole of the blessed Trinity, and with Him who is alone, by essence, the infinite Majesty, the King of Kings and the Lord of Lords, as the eldest daughter of the Father, Mother most tender of the Word, and spouse of predilection of the Holy Spirit...

"That is why the Church salutes her as Sovereign and Queen of the angels and saints, of the patriarchs and prophets, of the apostles and martyrs, of the confessors and virgins. That is why the Church proclaims her 'Queen of Heaven and of the Earth', 'glorious and most worthy Queen of the universe', 'Regina coelorum', 'gloriosa Regina mundi'. That is why she teaches us to invoke her, day and night, in the midst of our groanings and tears in our exile: 'Salve Regina...', 'Hail, Holy Queen, Mother of Mercy, hail, our life, our sweetness and our hope!' For her queenship is essentially maternal, and exclusively concerned with doing good.

"Is it not precisely this queenship which you have experienced? Have you not come here today to proclaim and acknowledge the remarkable benefits and the innumerable tokens of the tenderness which you have been granted by the maternal Heart of your august Queen? During four long years, the most terrible war which has ever ravaged the world prowled around your frontiers, but it never broke through them, owing above all to Our Lady who, from her throne of mercy, present here like a sublime watchtower in the centre of the country, took care of you and of your governments; she did not allow the war to touch you, and you were only permitted a conjecture of the unheard of calamities from which her protection preserved you.

"Yes, crown her Queen of peace and of the world, so that she may help the world to rediscover peace and to raise itself up from its ruins! Thus this crown, a symbol of love and gratitude for the past, and of faith and vassalage for the present, will also be, for the future, a crown of fidelity and hope. In crowning the image of Our Lady, you have signed and attested your faith in her Queenship, your loyal submission to her authority, your filial and constant correspondence to her love. You have done more: you have pledged yourselves, as crusaders, for the conquest or the reconquest of her kingdom, which is the kingdom of God; that is to say, you have obliged yourselves, in the sight of heaven and earth, to love her, to venerate her, to serve her and to imitate her, in order better to serve the divine King; and, at the same time, you have obliged yourselves to work so that she is loved, venerated and served around you, in your families, in society, in the entire world.

"In this decisive hour of history, just as the kingdom of evil, deploying an infernal strategy, uses every means and unleashes all its forces in order to destroy faith, morality and the Kingdom of God, in the same way the sons of light, the children of God, should employ everything, and all should employ themselves, to defend them, if we do not wish to witness a ruin infinitely more grave and more disastrous than all the material ruins accumulated during the war.

"In this struggle, there is no place for the neutral or

undecided. What is needed is an enlightened, convinced and fearless Catholicism, a Catholicism of faith and action, of opinions and works, in private as well as in public life, a Catholicism which may be resumed in the formula proclaimed four years ago at Fatima by the valiant Catholic Youth: 'Catholics one hundred per cent!'

"In the hope that our wishes will be favourably received by the Immaculate Heart of Mary, and will hasten the hour of her triumph and of the triumph of the kingdom of God, as a pledge of heavenly graces, to you, Venerable Brethren, and to all your clergy, to his Excellency, the President of the Republic, to the illustrious Head and to the members of the government, to the other civil and military authorities, to you all dear sons and dear daughters, pious pilgrims of Our Lady of Fatima, and to all those who are united with you in spirit in continental, insular and over-seas Portugal, we impart with all our love and all our paternal affection, the apostolic blessing."

Coming after the speech of 31 October 1942, this radio message marked a new advance in the official recognition of the apparitions of the Queen of Heaven at Fatima. Pius XII, in fact, had not hesitated to use the strongest expressions which no longer left any place for doubt: he openly spoke of the "prodigy of Fatima" and attributed to the Virgin of Fatima the miracle of peace from which Portugal had just profited. He evoked with enthusiasm the place of the apparitions: "this blessed oasis, impregnated with the supernatural", where one experiences in the most tangible manner the marvellous protection of the Immaculate Heart of Mary, "this Cova da Iria transformed into a gushing source of graces, physical prodigies, and even more, of miracles of the moral order", not only for Portugal, but for the whole Church and for the entire world.

The official closure of the tercentenary celebrations was due to take place at Lisbon on 8 December, the feast of the Immaculate Conception, and a procession covering more than 400 kilometres was organised. The statue of the Virgin of Fatima left the Capelinha on 22 November and was not due to return there until one month later, on Christmas Eve.

"The crowd extended for several kilometres along the route. There were never less than 2,000 pilgrims praying and singing; sometimes their number rose to 15,000." The streets were strewn with flowers and decorated with triumphal arches and banners. At night the people brought out chinese lanterns. "In the churches, there was nocturnal adoration of the Blessed Sacrament and early morning Masses and holy communion, preceding Mass on the public square or in the stadium, in front of immense crowds presided over by the local authorities. This was how it transpired in Leira, Batalha, Porto de Mos, Caldas da Rainha, Peniche, Bombarral..." (Canon Barthas, *Les Colombes de la Vierge*, 1977, pp.14-15).

It was during this triumphal journey towards the capital that there took place for the first time the famous "miracle of the doves". This marvellous occurrence soon caused such a stir that Cardinal Cerejeira appointed Father Domingos Fernandes to conduct a minute investigation into it, and this was published by the Cardinal as an appendix to the collection of his *Pastoral Works*. It is from this document that the following account is taken:

"On 1 December 1946, in the town of Bombarral, at the moment when the statue of Our Lady of Fatima was leaving for Cadaval, six doves were released by two young girls. Five of them settled on the plinth under the statue of Our Lady, and stayed there. As they left the town, three of them stayed on the plinth while the two others flew away. But these were caught and put back on the plinth, where they remained without moving until they reached Lousa, when they flew off and took refuge under a porch.

"The doves were seen by several thousand people,

during the second, third, fourth and fifth of December, at Cadaval, Torres Vedras, Mafra and Loures. Each day, a torchlight procession was organised at nightfall to escort the statue, and during the night the image remained in the church, always accompanied by crowds of believers. All this time the doves stayed on the plinth, huddled up close to the statue. During the night of 4 December, the procession which was escorting the statue of Our Lady arrived in pouring rain at the church of Loures. Although they were wet, the doves did not stir from their position huddled up close to the image." (*Obras Pastorais*, vol. III, pp. 231-233).

Cardinal Cerejeira himself commented on this remarkable phenomenon:

"These doves recently took up their position at the feet of the white image of Our Lady of Fatima, almost hidden under her garment, amidst the flowers. Ten of thousands of people saw them there, pressed up one against the other, facing the gentle image, with their little beaks touching the hem of her garment, as if they wanted to kiss the feet of the Madonna. Occasionally they would fly off for a few brief moments. But they were so content to be perched there that neither the noise of the crowds, nor the sound of the music, nor the explosions of the fireworks, nor the rain, nor the wind, nor the cold, nor the day, nor the night, nor the cascade of petals or bouquets, nothing was able to dislodge them from their position." (Ibid, pp. 222-223).

They were still there when they got to Lisbon. From 5 to 7 December the statue of the Virgin remained in the vast and recently constructed church dedicated to Our Lady of Fatima.

"The next day, which was the first Friday of the month, one of the doves flew up to perch on her crown, and there, in a posture facing the altar, it held its wings open during the communion of some 3,000 of the faithful." (Canon Barthas, op. cit, p. 17).

On the night of 7 December, the vigil of the feast of

the Immaculate Conception, the statue was escorted to the cathedral. Two of the doves remained in the church and the third alone followed the Madonna, who was escorted over the six kilometres by an immense torchlight procession of some 100,000 men! On 8 December, pontifical high Mass was celebrated at the cathedral, and in the afternoon there took place the official consecration of Portugal to the Immaculate Heart of Mary in the presence of the Head of State, Marshal Carmona, together with Salazar and all the members of the government. Finally, a solemn Te Deum was sung.

Pope Pius XII in the course of proclaiming the
infallible definition of the dogma of the Assumption of
the Most Holy Virgin.

Pope Pius XII welcomes the pilgrim Virgin of Fatima in St. Peter's basilica.

Chapter IX

FATIMA EMBRACES THE WORLD, 1947-1956

The Great Return had proved such an outstanding success in France that the same methods were soon adopted throughout Europe and the entire world. A brochure entitled 'Peregrinatio Mariae', which soon ran into millions of copies, defined the spirit of the Great Return:

"It is the triumphant passage from parish to parish of an image of the Madonna, in an uninterrupted succession of religious manifestations, with the salutary object of stirring up the mass of the faithful and leading them to rediscover in an inspired way their eucharistic and Marian piety, and the sincere and open practice of a real Christian life. More briefly, it is a spiritual movement for the masses to bring about the Great Return of souls to Jesus through Mary. This Marian route has, henceforth, a famous and unforgettable precedent in the Great Return that took place in France, and which was the greatest contemporary event in the religious life of that country. It has acquired such importance that it has become the admiration of the Catholic world, which is being drawn to imitate it." (Father L. Devineau, OMI, op.cit., p.163).

Marian routes sprang up all over Italy, amidst extraordinary scenes. In Milan, for example, "the passage of Mary aroused quite incredible enthusiasm... More than 100,000 people had assembled to greet the Queen of Milan. Never had such a huge crowd been seen before. His Eminence Cardinal Schuster gave an address of historic significance."(ibid., pp. 163-164).

In Canada, a national Marian Congress had been arranged at Ottawa for mid-June 1947. By way of

preparing the faithful, a Great Return was organised
with the statue of Our Lady of the Cape, patron of
Canada. This Marian route of the "Ark of the
Covenant", as it was happily known, aroused a vast
movement of fervour, just as it had done in Europe. On
19 June, Pope Pius XII sent a stirring radio message to
the Congress, in which he recalled the marvellous
devotion to the Immaculate which had flourished since 8
December 1635, when the first French missionaries had
consecrated to Mary all the existing and future missions
to Canada.

Next it was the turn of Hungary. Despite all sorts of
attempts to frustrate him by the Russians, Cardinal
Mindszenty had been able to attend the Marian Congress
in Ottawa. He came back from it with a grandiose
project for a Marian year to be extended throughout all
Hungary, which the hierarchy received with enthusiasm.

"It was at Esztergom, on 15 August 1947," the
Cardinal recalled in his Memoirs, "that I opened this
Holy Year. All the bishops of Hungary and 60,000
pilgrims took part in the ceremony" (p.169). On the
same day, throughout the whole country 1,500,000 of
the faithful poured into the various places of pilgrimage
and sanctuaries dedicated to the Virgin, and hundreds of
thousands of the faithful attended the various congresses
and ceremonies which took place almost without
interruption during the rest of the year.

"The Communists spared no efforts to disrupt the
services and meetings and prevent the people from
hearing the sermons and addresses, particularly those of
the Cardinal. At railway stations, tickets were not sold
to pilgrims; buses and lorries were commandeered;
movement from one region to another was banned,
ostensibly to prevent the spread of infectious disease.
On the pretext that they were endangering road and rail
safety, groups of pilgrims were broken up; house and
open-air Masses were drowned by the roaring of tractor
engines; the use of-loud speakers and microphones was

forbidden; water and electricity supplies were cut off, etc." (Mgr. J. Kozi-Horvath, *Cardinal Mindszenty*, p.27). Despite all this, 4,600,000 of the faithful took part in the solemnities and pilgrimages of the Marian Year in Hungary.

Still in 1947, on 12 October Pope Pius XII sent a radio message on the Virgin Mary to the Marian Congress of Argentina at the sanctuary of Lujan, and on 7 December he sent a further radio message to the members of the international congress of Marian congregations, who were meeting at Barcelona. But without doubt the two most important Marian interventions by the Sovereign Pontiff in this year were the canonisations of Saint Louis-Marie Grignion de Montfort and of St. Catherine Labouré.

On 20 July, Saint Louis de Montfort was raised to the supreme honours of the altar, and the next day, in an address to the pilgrims who had come to Rome for this canonisation, the Pope recalled the life of the great Breton saint:

"His great secret for drawing souls and giving them to Jesus, was devotion to Mary... All his action was founded on her; in her was all his assurance, and he could not have found a more efficacious arm at such a period. To the austerity without joy, the sombre terror and the proud depression of Jansenism, he opposed the filial, confident, ardent, affective and effective love of the devout servant of Mary towards her who is the refuge of sinners, the Mother of divine grace, our life, our sweetness, our hope. And our advocate also..."

The canonisation of Saint Louis-Marie, the prophet of the final triumph and reign of the Immaculate in preparation for the reign of her Son, was a decision of the highest importance.

One week later on 27 July, Pope Pius XII canonised the seer of the rue du Bac, "the messenger of the Immaculate". In his address to the pilgrims, he recalled the requests which the Virgin had charged her to

transmit: "...to submerge the whole world with a deluge
of little medals bearing all the corporal and spiritual
mercies of the Immaculate, and to found a pious
association of Children of Mary, to protect and sanctify
young girls".

While he was tireless in encouraging true devotion to
Mary, Pope Pius XII was also capable of defending it
firmly against its enemies, when the occasion required
it. Thus, in his masterly encyclical on the holy liturgy
of 20 November 1947, *Mediator Dei*, he insisted on the
pre-eminent cult due to the Virgin Mary our Mother,
who "gives us her Son, and with Him all the help which
we need, for God willed that we should have everything
by Mary".

Among other pastoral directives, he warned the
bishops: **"Do not yield to the demands that are made
by certain people in the supposed interests of a
liturgical revival, or on the false assumption that
only liturgical practices have any value or
efficacy... and that devotion to the Blessed Virgin
Mother of God, which is regarded by the saints as a
sign of predestination, should be so neglected,
especially in youth, as gradually to fade away and
disappear.** These are poisoned fruits growing on
infected branches of a healthy tree, and they are most
damaging to Christian piety; they must be cut off, so
that the life-giving sap may nourish only the fruit that is
sweet and good...

"There are certain other pious practises which,
though not belonging strictly to the liturgy, nevertheless
enjoy a special importance and dignity, such that they
are regarded as raised to liturgical rank, and have
received repeated approval from this Apostolic See and
the Episcopate. Among these are special devotions to
the Virgin Mother of God during the month of May...
**It would therefore be damaging as well as erroneous
to take it upon oneself to change all these practices
of piety**, and to try to fit them into the framework of

the liturgy" (Pope Pius XII, *Mediator Dei*, Nos. 188,194, 196).

Finally, 1947 was also the year in which the world voyage of Our Lady of Fatima began. For more than ten years, as from 13 May 1947, the Immaculate Mediatrix was to travel almost continuously throughout the world and accomplish a "pilgrimage of marvels", as Pius XII was soon to describe it.

The idea of a Great Return of Our Lady of Fatima throughout all Europe had little by little taken root. Finally it was proposed that the Pilgrim Virgin would go to Maastricht in Holland, to preside over the great Marian Congress of the three countries which were shortly to be formed into the Benelux.

"The evening before they were due to set forth, the organisers took a beautiful statue, which they had specially bought to be carried on the route, to Sister Lucia, who at that time was at Vila Nova de Gaia. She advised them to go and ask the Bishop of Leiria for the statue which he kept in his sitting-room, for which she herself had personally guided the hand of the artist, José Ferreira Thedim, and to ask him if he would agree to exchange it for the one which they had just bought. Lucia added: 'This Virgin will travel right up to the frontiers of Russia, and there it will be necessary to offer up many prayers so that she reaches Moscow. And after she has finished her pilgrimage, it would be as well to offer the image to the Holy Father.'

"With his customary goodness, Mgr. da Silva abandoned his beautiful statue, and the next day, 13 May, she was crowned at the Cova da Iria in front an immense crowd of pilgrims by the Bishop of Evora" (Canon Barthas, Fatima, *Merveille du XXe siécle*, pp.275-276).

The procession set off in the afternoon, and although the programme had provided for a rapid transit through Portugal, everywhere Our Lady was greeted with the same enthusiasm and fervour that had been seen six months earlier when she travelled from Fatima to Lisbon.

The reception of the Virgin of Fatima by Spain surpassed all expectations. "The first passage of the Pilgrim Virgin into Spain," wrote Father Alonso, "was, without exaggeration, an apotheosis... There followed a month of enthusiastic receptions in the course of which the ecclesiastical and civil authorities and innumerable crowds of the faithful demonstrated to the Virgin of Fatima their filial homage of love and veneration." At Valladolid, the seat of Mgr. Garcia y Garcia, it was a magnificent triumph, attended by more than 100,000 of the faithful!

"Throughout Spain, the sheriffs of the villages which she traversed piously laid their staff of office at the feet of the Virgin; every two hundred metres, two civil guards presented arms to her; the bishops received the Virgin upon entering their diocese and went to present her to the bishop of the adjoining diocese; cinemas and theatres closed for the visit of Our Lady; everywhere the normal working day was brought to a standstill; the event occupied the most prominent place in the newspapers, etc."

Confessions and communions, processions, rosaries, holy hours of reparation, and consecrations to the Immaculate Heart of Mary followed one after another. "The graces of marvellous cures multiplied prodigiously", states Father Alonso. Finally Our Lady reached San Sebastian and, on 18 June, Hendaya. Owing to the scandalous blockade of Franco's Spain, which had been decided upon following the Yalta and Potsdam agreements, the frontier between France and Spain was still closed, as it had been for the last eleven years. The reception which France gave to the Virgin of Fatima was distinctly less enthusiastic than that accorded to her by Spain. No mention of her arrival had been made in the press, and eye-witnesses had the impression that the French police had been ordered not to allow her to enter the country. But, confronted by the Bishop of Vittoria of Spain, and the Bishop of Bayonne of France, who gave each other a friendly embrace, and by a crowd on both sides of the border who were singing the same hymns to the Virgin, "the commissioner of police resorted to the subterfuge of allowing her to enter by issuing a customs clearance note for Belgium, as if she was a common parcel".

On 2 August she arrived at the Belgian frontier, and she was received with great enthusiasm by the cities of Tournai, Charleroi, Namur, Beauraing, Liége and Verviers. On 1 September, she entered Holland to preside over the Marian Congress of Maastricht, for which Pius XII once again broadcast a radio message. At Luxembourg her reception was even more fervent: 100,000 communions out of a population of 250,000 inhabitants! She met with the same success at Malines, Louvain and Brussels, where 300,000 faithful came out to greet her. After a tour of Flanders, the Pilgrim Virgin embarked to return to Portugal.

In but a few months, what a torrent of graces she poured out on all those who had chosen to honour her! Mgr. da Silva declared: **"Not one of us had foreseen the marvellous things which began to happen as soon as the statue left the Cova da Iria."** Canon Barthas notes that the news of her visit to Spain and the Benelux, and of the marvels the Virgin worked on her route, rapidly became common knowledge, and so letters began to reach the Bishop of Fatima from every direction requesting a visit from the Pilgrim Virgin.

On 13 October 1947, a statue of the Virgin of Fatima left the Cova da Iria for the airport of Lisbon, where she was installed in the place of honour in a plane bound for America. She was solemnly received at the sanctuary of Our Lady of the Cape, where she was blessed by Mgr. Vachon, Archbishop of Ottawa, in front of 100,000 faithful. This was followed by a ceremony of coronation, consecration to her Immaculate Heart, a vigil of prayers, and at midnight, Mass in the cathedral and in 124 churches of the diocese!

On 8 December, in the spectacular setting of the Niagara Falls, she crossed the border between Canada and the United States. The Archbishop of Buffalo received the venerated image from the hands of the Bishop of Hamilton. At the cathedral where she was received, 200,000 people came to pray to her, whereas the town only numbered 50,000 Catholics! And scenes like this were repeated in all the dioceses and parishes of the United States where she was received.

As a result of this Marian route in America, still in this same year of 1947, Mgr. Colgan, who at that time was parish priest of Plainfield, aided by a young journalist called John Haffert, who was full of drive and enthusiasm, founded the Blue Army of Our Lady of Fatima, in order to propagate the Message of Fatima and work towards its realisation. The programme was simple: daily rosary; devotion to the Immaculate Heart of Mary with its two components – reparation and consecration; wearing the scapular of Our Lady of Mount Carmel; and the fulfilment of the duties of one's state in life, in a spirit of penance. At this time the object of the Blue Army was to obtain peace for the world by the conversion of Russia, and it propagated the authentic Message of Fatima, without omission, and without watering it down or contaminating it with suspect revelations which were quite foreign to the message transmitted by Sister Lucia. The movement achieved such a rapid success that it already numbered one million members by 1950 !

Meanwhile the missionary Virgin left her Capelinha in October of the same year to travel throughout the south of Portugal, which was the most dechristianized part of the country. Even in those regions, the white image of the Immaculate was received with moving enthusiasm, and she sowed graces of all kinds among the people. Whereas, during the preceding months that the image was travelling in Spain, in France, in the Benelux, and in America, in spite of the affluence and fervour of the crowds, the astonishing miracle of the doves did not once take place, here, in the land of Holy Mary, it was renewed in a startling fashion. To take just one example out of the many that could be cited:

"In the village of Gafanheiros, a man in the crowd protested that the birds were attached to the plinth, and that he would only believe they were free if his own would go and join them. He was invited to try it out, so he gave several doves to a lady and asked her to release them only when he told her. This was done when the plinth was a dozen or more metres away. All the birds flew off to alight on the plinth, and they remained there the whole day".

On 2 July 1948, Pope Pius XII wrote a letter to Father Ranson, S.J., the director of the Great Return in France, which clearly reveals the thinking of the Sovereign Pontiff on the devotion to the Immaculate Heart of Mary, then gathering pace throughout the world:

"You have indeed understood and put into practice our instruction to persevere, as is proved by the numerous manifestations in public or private, creating a spectacle which delights us, and by means of which consecration to the Immaculate Heart of Mary is developing and intensifying in all sectors of society. Besides, have we not ourselves given the signal for this to happen, as the providential complement of the consecration of the human race to the Sacred Heart of Jesus?

"We have said it before and we wish to repeat it: amidst the dark night which still hangs over the world, we see the beginnings of a dawn, the infallible messenger of the Son of truth, of justice and of love. It is indeed no small sign of hope and comfort to contemplate this extraordinary impetus, in this ravaged and anxious generation, to 'return' to the source of the living waters

which spring up abundantly from the Sacred Hearts of
Jesus and Mary.

"So we congratulate you on taking this salvific Marian
devotion to heart, on propagating it all around you, and
on making it the principal lever of your apostolate. We
believe that in it is to be found the assured pledge of the
conversion of sinners, the perseverance and progress of
the faithful, and the re-establishment of a true peace
between all the nations and with God" (Cited in Father
Devineau, op. cit., pp.6-8).

**"The cult of the Immaculate Heart of Mary is
developing marvellously from day to day"**, Pope Pius
XII observed with joy on 19 September 1948. In the two
years alone from 1948 to 1949, no fewer than eleven
Marian Congresses took place. By December 1948, the
Marian Congregations representing the pious and
apostolic movements working among the laity numbered
some 8,000,000 members, drawn from more than
75,000 different groups. Pius XII encouraged their
development, and he also multiplied his allusions to the
Immaculate Heart of Mary in his addresses. For
example, in his letter to the Polish episcopate on 18
January 1948 he wrote: "The necessity to find one's
refuge and to receive one's strength in this sacred Heart
appears more pressing than ever today. For our
heavenly Mother does not only shine with gentleness,
like the morning star, but she is also this strong Woman
who, to avenge the rights of her divine Son, has on
several occasions risen up in the Church, 'terrible as an
army in battle array' ".

Nor did the Pope miss any opportunity of recalling
the consecration of the human race to the Immaculate
Heart of Mary which he carried out in 1942, "at a
moment when all the resources and hopes of humanity
seemed in vain and unable to appease a conflict of such
gravity". On 1 May 1948, in his encyclical *Auspicia
Quaedam*, he insisted: "If the circumstances are
opportune, we wish that this consecration (to the

Immaculate Heart of Mary) should be carried out in the dioceses, and also in each parish and in the families, and we are confident that this private and public consecration will bring down an abundance of heavenly blessings and favours." Soon the city of Rome was solemnly consecrated to the Immaculate Heart of Mary, and meanwhile, as active preparations were being made for the definition of the dogma of the Assumption, the white image of the Virgin of Fatima was pursuing her missionary route across the world.

From 23 to 30 May 1948, the Pilgrim Virgin visited Madrid, and there resulted in the words of Father da Fonseca, "the most extraordinary apotheosis which was ever recorded in the annals of Fatima, and certainly one of the most splendid ceremonies which was ever accorded to the Most Holy Virgin." That year the Bishop of Madrid, Mgr. Eijo y Garay, was celebrating the silver jubilee of his episcopate in the capital. He decided to turn this event into an act of homage to the Virgin Mary, by arranging a Marian Congress for the last nine days of May. Accordingly, he asked Mgr. da Silva to lend him the statue which was venerated at the Capelinha, and as the Bishop of Leiria refused, Mgr. Eijo y Garay insisted by passing his request through diplomatic channels. Mgr. da Silva acceded to the request presented by the Foreign Ministry of Lisbon, and in the event he came to the Congress himself, accompanied by the Bishop of Gurza and Cardinal Cerejeira.

The population of Madrid at that time numbered 800,000 inhabitants, but when the Virgin of Fatima entered the city on 23 May she found that 1,500,000 of the faithful had come to greet her! It was the greatest assemblage which had ever been seen in her honour. She was carried to the Plaza Major, and then to the cathedral where, day and night, she was besieged by the faithful. In the following days, the missionary Virgin was taken to the suburbs of the city, where, says Father Alonso, "the people exhibited a tireless fervour, which had never been seen before in these parts, and graces of conversion and healing were multiplied prodigiously."

Father da Fonseca reports that the wife and daughter of the Head of State, General Franco, came to visit Our Lady every day in the different churches to which she was taken. In the afternoon of 26 May, the image was taken to the residence of the Head of State, who received her, in the company of all his family and the civil and military staff of his house, in the chapel of the Palace, which was richly decorated with flowers. The rosary was recited, followed by the singing of the Salve Regina. Afterwards, the doors of the chapel were opened and the people crowded in to show their love for the Virgin. Our Lady's statue also made special visits to the seminary and to the university.

"Wherever she passed in the streets", says Father Alonso, "the enthusiastic crowds acclaimed her noisily. But the most remarkable manifestations took place on the Plaza de la Armeria, which had been transformed into a royal altar for the Virgin. The Mass of 29 May, in the presence of 10,000 sick surrounded by a large crowd, with its succession of miraculous cures, was a peak of religious significance which it is impossible to describe.

"The visit finally ended with pontifical High Mass on Sunday 30 May, when the patriarch of Madrid officiated, assisted by the cardinals of Toledo and Lisbon. Special seats had been set aside for the Caudillo, his wife and daughter, and for all the members of the government. Numerous prelates and other civil and military authorities were also present."

The address of Cardinal Cerejeira on this occasion was particularly eloquent.

"The image of Our Lady of Fatima," he declared, "recalls to my mind the last merciful intervention of the Immaculate Heart of Mary. Her voice is the piercing cry of a mother who sees a fathomless abyss of misery opening up in front of her poor frightened children. It is an appeal, it is a hope, it is salvation in this apocalyptic hour. Fatima has become the hope of the nations... **What precisely is the message of Fatima? I think that it may be resumed in these terms: it is the revelation of the Immaculate Heart of Mary to the present world...** I repeat what I have often said: **Fatima is to the cult of the Immaculate Heart of Mary what Paray-le-Monial was to the cult of the Sacred Heart of Jesus. In a certain way, Fatima is the continuation, or rather the conclusion of Paray-le-Monial: Fatima reunites these two Hearts whom God Himself has united in the divine work of Redemption.**"

When he returned to Lisbon, the cardinal patriarch confessed that he had found an extraordinary spirit of faith and devotion in Spain: "Spain surpassed everything that could have been imagined. What I saw at Madrid nearly blinded me. I saw the Catholic soul of Spain in its finest manifestation... The Virgin gave proof of her love for Spain by the miracles which took place there" (Father Alonso, *Fatima, Espana, Rusia*, pp. 108-110).

For his part, the Bishop of Madrid wrote to Mgr. da Silva to thank him for lending the statue of Our Lady from the Capelinha: "I am unable to find words sufficiently expressive to tell Your Excellency... the marvel of the passage of the thrice-blessed image across the streets and the squares of Madrid, during these nine days in which we had the happiness to have her in our possession. **Days of heaven ! There was an over-powering, triumphant wave of the supernatural, beyond all human expression !... Only Mary can draw hearts in this way and win them to her Divine Son.** From the moment she entered my diocese, she never stopped conquering souls and collecting crowds of hundreds of thousands of the faithful, even poor unbelievers: all came to pay homage to her image, acclaiming her, weeping, praying, and singing pious hymns. Never, never had Madrid seen anything comparable !... Throughout the whole country, the only conversation was of Our Lady of Fatima, of her passage through Madrid, of her numerous miracles, of her innumerable conversions... I would exchange the twenty-five years of my apostolate here for these nine days... Throughout this period, the priests never left the confessional. The parish priests of the suburbs told me that more than forty per cent of their penitents who asked for confession had not been to the sacrament for the last fifteen, twenty or thirty years, etc". (Canon Barthas, *Fatima et les destins du monde*, pp. 56-57).

We have omitted to mention that nowhere more than in Catholic Spain was the miracle of the doves more startling. "Throughout the whole Congress, whether she was in the streets or in the churches, the Virgin was never seen without this white escort of honour, and often it was very numerous". Some moving examples of this phenomenon are quoted in the book by Canon Barthas entitled *Les Colombes de la Vierge*. Let us hear the story of Father José Luis Castilla, the director of the review *Reinado Social de Sagrado Corazon* (The Social Reign of the Sacred Heart):

"May the Virgin forgive me, but I wanted to discover for myself whether the doves were free or attached to her, so that I could report it to the readers of *Reinado Social*. I climbed up the steps of the altar, on the Plaza de la Armeria. I approached the doves and tried to pick them up, but they did not want to leave their Queen. They defended themselves valiantly, and pecked my hands angrily. I succeeded in getting hold of a few and I threw them as far away as I could with all my strength. (Father Castilla was a veritable Hercules!). They barely went an arm's length, wheeled round sharply, and flew back like arrows to the throne of Mary...

"Father Vermeer, O.M.I., who accompanied the statue, told us that a young girl who was ill in bed was very sorry that she could not get up in order to admire the doves. When the procession passed in front of her room, a dove entered it through the open window, settled for some time in full view of the girl on the end of her bed, and left to rejoin its companions after the whole household had commented with delight on its visit."(op.cit. , pp.38-40).

The following year, on 4 May 1949, Father Gorricho had an audience with the Caudillo, and proposed the solemn consecration of Spain to the Immaculate Heart of Mary. Franco replied: "That is what I want! But it should come from the hierarchy!" The bishops took a long time to make up their minds, but the consecration was finally done, however, in the Marian Year of 1954. Let us note in passing that, on 26 October 1949, during an official visit to Portugal, Franco himself went on pilgrimage to Fatima. Photographs show him kneeling at the feet of the Virgin of the Capelinha, assisting at Mass with his missal in his hand.

It is undeniable that Spain experienced an incomparable Catholic renaissance during those years. Father Alonso states categorically that it was a period of authentic re-christianisation of Spain, and his book gives solid proofs to substantiate this claim. The seminaries and religious colleges filled up and new ones had to be constructed. The popular missions multiplied and bore fruit; attendance at the sacraments increased notably. Once again, numerous Spanish missionaries left for countries all over the world, especially to South America. With reason Father Alonso attributes this marvellous expansion to the head of the Church, Pope Pius XII, and to Her who was "the soul and the spiritual motor" of this great movement of return to God, "this little white pilgrim and missionary Virgin, who traversed each and every one of the regions of Spain", in the years following 1948. (op. cit.,pp. 7,138).

The Pilgrim Virgin of Fatima not only travelled the roads of Spain, but those of the entire world. Still with the same miraculous success, in April 1948 she visited the island of Madeira, Cape Verde and Portuguese

Guinea. In June she went to the Azores, in July to Sao Tomé and then to Angola. Throughout all these Portuguese provinces, she was always accompanied in the same miraculous fashion by the doves.

On 30 September, the Virgin left for Mozambique, and it was very remarkable, by contrast, as Canon Barthas observes, that throughout all Eastern Africa and in all the countries where the Moslems predominated, the gracious winged guard of doves was no longer seen at the sides of the white statue, despite the fact that the Moslems were often more numerous and sometimes even more fervent in their acclamations than the Catholics... Magnificent celebrations marked her passage through Rhodesia, Kenya, Tanganyika and Uganda, etc. But nowhere were the doves seen to give the slightest sign of veneration to the Pilgrim Virgin... She travelled through Eritrea, Sudan, Egypt and Lybia, but never were any doves to be seen beside her.

The statue of Our Lady returned to Portugal in July 1949, and left Lisbon again by aeroplane for Bombay on 24 November. From Bombay she went to Goa, and after visiting India she was then was received in triumph in Pakistan. She returned to Bombay, visited Ceylon, and finally returned to the Cova da Iria on 13 August 1950. Meanwhile several statues were traversing Vietnam, having been bought by the vicars-apostolic of Hanoi, Phat-Diem and Haiphong while on a pilgrimage to Fatima. In 1951, she was to set out for Australia and Oceania.

In his radio message to the pilgrims at Fatima on 13 October 1951, Pope Pius XII referred to this world-wide pilgrimage of the Virgin of Fatima, and said:

"After her passage, in America just as in Europe, in Africa and India, in Indonesia and Australia, heaven rained down blessings, and marvels of grace multiplied everywhere, to such an extent that we can hardly believe what our eyes are seeing."

"If what I say to you is done, many souls will be saved and there will be peace", said Our Lady of Fatima on 13 July 1917.

It is important to underline the fact that the Virgin of Fatima continued to fulfil – and with such liberality – this marvellous promise of salvation for souls and peace for the nations in these last years of the pontificate of Pius XII. In Portugal, in Austria, in Spain, and wherever people strove to correspond with love and with eagerness to the great requests of her Immaculate Heart, she granted her graces of conversion and peace. As the all-powerful Mediatrix, she is able to distribute these graces to all souls throughout the entire world.

The "land of Holy Mary" was the first to profit from the fruits of these extraordinary graces, as Cardinal Cerejeira recognised in a conference which he gave on "the situation of the Church in Portugal" on 29 November 1956:

"I note first of all the fact – for which we can never sufficiently give thanks – of the peace, the liberty and the renewal of the Church in Portugal... Those who, half a century ago, took up the axe of persecution against the old tree in whose shelter took refuge all those who believed, hoped and loved, will never understand how the decrepit and barren trunk has become green again, has sprouted branches, flowers and fruits, and once again shelters its own children. I should add that we ourselves do not fully understand it. One cannot talk of this marvellous renovation without beginning by mentioning the miracle of Fatima in 1917. The apparition of Our Lady of Fatima was indeed, for Portugal, like the rainbow which, according to the story in the Bible, appeared in the sky after the flood: a new era of peace was about to begin."

Throughout his entire pontificate, Pius XII supported, encouraged and blessed this miraculous restoration, of which Cardinal Cerejeira at the head of the Church and Salazar at the head of the State were the providential instruments. The Pope said publicly of Salazar: "I bless him with all my heart, and my most ardent wish is that he will be able to bring to a successful conclusion his work of national restoration, both materially and spiritually." (Quoted by Plancard d'Assac, *Salazar*, p.228). It should also be noted that the seer of Fatima held the same opinion about the Head of State. "It is known how cordial were the relations between Lucia and Salazar", stated Father Messias dias Coelho. Indeed, Salazar visited Lucia several times at the Carmel of Coimbra and there was an exchange of letters between them. And as long as Portugal, united behind its providential leaders, remained faithful to its heavenly patron, it continued to benefit from her miraculous protection. This was seen yet again in the summer of 1954, when all of a sudden Goa was gravely threatened.

Openly encouraged by Prime Minister Nehru of India and his government, so-called "volunteers" surrounded the Portuguese colony of Goa and proclaimed that they would liberate it on 15 August. But they had not counted on the "spiritual mobilisation" of the Portuguese people. In churches and sanctuaries throughout the country, they organised vigils of prayer and novenas for peace. At Goa and Lisbon, they exposed the relics of Saint Francis-Xavier, and publicly and solemnly invoked his protection, as well as that of Saint John de Britto, a Portuguese missionary to India. A million pilgrims left on foot from Lisbon, on 10 August, arriving at Fatima on the 14th after marching day and night. Suddenly, in the most unforeseen way, Nehru ordered the police and the army to prevent the volunteers from crossing the frontier of Portuguese Goa.

The lesson is clear. If on the one hand God grants His miraculous help to a whole people united in prayer behind their leaders, on the other hand, when their fervour has died down, their confidence fails, and even their own shepherds no longer seem to believe in their own cause, then God abandons men to their own weakness.

There is the remarkable example of Austria. It is well-known that at the end of the Second World War, part of Austrian territory was occupied by the Soviets. What is less well-known is the almost miraculous manner in which this Catholic state was suddenly delivered from the yoke of Moscow.

For the USSR, Austria obviously represented a stronghold in the heart of Europe, on account of its strategic situation and its oil-wells. But in 1955, in an entirely unexpected development, Moscow agreed to completely withdraw its forces of occupation, thereby restoring full independence to Austria, which regained its 1938 frontiers. What had happened? All this came about because between 700,000 and 1,000,000 people, that is to say, between 10 and 12% of the population, had signed a promise to say the rosary every day and to fulfil the wishes of Our Lady of Fatima.

Theresa Neumann, the stigmatist of Konnersreuth, had no doubt at all about that: "It was definitely the prayers and the numerous rosaries of the Austrian people which obtained their freedom and complete deliverance from the Russia domination", she declared in 1962, shortly before her death.

(Just as this book was going to be typeset I received, quite unexpectedly, a copy of a book which brings a valuable clarification to this story. It is entitled *He Taught Millions to Pray*, and is the life of Father Peter Pavlicek, OFM, the Austrian Franciscan who organised this rosary campaign to liberate his country from the Soviet yoke. The information which follows has been extracted from pages 57 to 64 of this work – note by T. Tindal-Robertson).

After the end of the Second World War, the Austrian government had vainly made repeated attempts to negotiate an agreement with Russia, whereby Austria would be enabled to regain its independence as a

democratic state according to the agreements which had
been worked out earlier at Yalta. Things worsened in
1954 when Molotov, the then Soviet Foreign Minister,
demanded that Austria declare itself willing to retain
Russian troops in the country until the German question
had been clarified. This meant, in effect, that the
Russians would remain there on an indefinite basis.

Meanwhile Father Peter, who realised that only
prayer could achieve the liberation of his country, had
founded a Rosary Crusade which by about 1950
numbered some 80,000 members. Their annual
torchlight procession was held on the Feast of the Holy
Name of Mary, 17 September. This feast had been
extended to the universal Church by Pope Innocent XI in
1683, after the siege of Vienna and the glorious victory
of Sobieski over the Turks on 12 September of the same
year.

In September 1950, for the first time their annual
procession was led by the Federal Chancellor of Austria,
praying the rosary, and at his suggestion the next year
he was also joined by the Cardinal. In 1952 the statue of
Our Lady, which Father Peter had brought from
Fatima, was solemnly crowned, and from 1953 onwards
the procession was led through the streets of the capital
by the Foreign Minister as well as the Federal Chancellor
– praying for peace and freedom for Austria.

In 1954 Father Peter wrote to the Federal Chancellor
in the name of his Rosary Crusaders, whose numbers
had now swollen to some 450,000 members, requesting
the re-instatement of the Feast of the Immaculate
Conception as a public holiday. For centuries this feast
had been a public holiday in Austria, and in 1947
Cardinal Innitzer had solemnly renewed the vow to retain
the feast. But just two years later the holiday was
abolished, on the pretext that as Austria was in such a
reduced economic state, the country could not afford an
additional holiday. Father Peter was convinced that this
was a betrayal of Austria's promise to Our Lady, and

that she could not be asked to intercede until her feast
was restored. 1954 was a particularly appropriate year to
request its re-instatement, as it had been declared a
Marian Year by Pope Pius XII, and it was also the one
hundredth anniversary of the dogmatic definition of the
Immaculate Conception. "The current Marian Year",
said Father Peter in his letter to the Chancellor, "offers a
unique opportunity to erase Austria's blemish of this
breach of faith..."

The petition was granted, and it can hardly be
without significance that Father Peter's letter was written
almost exactly one year before the completely unforeseen
conclusion of the treaty with Russia.

One day early in 1955, Chancellor Raab telephoned
Father Peter and asked him to get his members to pray as
never before. Shortly afterwards, a delegation from the
Austrian government was invited to Moscow, and the
formal negotiations began on 13 April 1955. **It was on
13 May** 1955 that the news was announced over the
radio that the Russians were willing to withdraw and sign
a peace treaty with the country. **Has there ever been
an occasion, before or since, when the Russians
have voluntarily withdrawn their troops from an
occupied country?**

The treaty was signed in Castle Belvedere on 15 May
1955, and a traditional rosary procession was held on the
Feast of the Holy Name of Mary at the Heldenplatz, in
thanksgiving. It was attended by the Chancellor and
Foreign Minister and numerous public personalities, and
in his address Chancellor Raab declared openly that he
believed their freedom had been won by the prayers of
Father Peter and his Rosary Crusaders: "...To those
Catholics who have joined this Crusade... I, as Federal
Chancellor, wish to express my sincere thanks for the
love, loyalty and spirit of sacrifice you have shown. I
ask this immense number of Austria's faithful Catholics
to remain true to their faith and unswerving in their
prayers... But for today we want to send up a joyful

prayer to Heaven and end it with the words: 'We are free! Mary, we thank you!'".

But it was above all in Spain, during the pontificate of Pius XII and under the protection of the Virgin of Fatima, that there took place a marvellous Catholic renaissance, in a spirit of perfect harmony between the two powers of the Church and the State. After her triumph in Madrid in May 1948, the Pilgrim Virgin of Fatima continued to travel throughout the dioceses of Spain, and everywhere she aroused the same enthusiasm and produced the same fruits of conversion and renewed fervour.

At the closing ceremonies of the 35th International Eucharistic Congress at Barcelona, on 1 June 1952, during the solemn Mass celebrated by Cardinal Tedeschini, the pontifical legate, General Franco read out a magnificent proclamation by which he consecrated Spain to the Most Holy Sacrament.

On 27 August 1953, a concordat exemplary in every detail was signed between the Holy See and Spain, according full and entire recognition to the rights and privileges of the Catholic Church, which was proclaimed "the only religion of the Spanish nation". This agreement finally put an official seal on a whole host of restorative measures which had been taken by General Franco in the years following his victory over the Communists.

"It re-established the Church in its privileged position of the past, acclaimed Catholicism as the religion of the State, recalled the Society of Jesus which had been driven out of Spain by the Republic, made the study of religion obligatory in schools and universities, repealed the law of divorce and gave legal recognition to religious marriage... For a long time the Catholic Church had not been treated with such respect and honour in Spain.

"There is no mystification or deceit about this matter," General Franco declared to the Cortes in 1953. "If we are Catholics, we are Catholics who also accept all the obligations which derive from this fact. For those nations that are Catholic, the questions of faith are foremost among the obligations of the state. The salvation or loss of souls, the rebirth or decline of faith, the expansion or the reduction of the true faith - these are problems of primary importance to which one cannot be indifferent." (Quoted in C. Martin, *Franco, Soldat et Chef d'État*, p. 394).

Finally, on 12 October 1954, during the Marian Congress of Saragossa, General Franco, speaking in the name of the whole nation, and kneeling at the feet of the Virgin of Pilar, read out an admirable consecration of Spain to the Immaculate Heart of Mary. The following brief extracts are taken from the account of this consecration, which is published in full in Father Alonso's book *Fatima, Espana, Rusia* (pp. 120-123):

"August Mother of God and compassionate Mother of men, on this soil of Saragossa watered by the blood of martyrs, and near your sacred pillar, the pledge of your predilection and symbol of the unquenchable faith of your people, we come here to fulfil a duty of love and of gratitude.

"Divine revelation teaches us, O Lady, that your Son, Our Lord, was delivered up to death to save us, because He loved us; and since the heart is the symbol and the mark of love, we adore the Divine Heart of Jesus, to whom our nation has been solemnly and officially consecrated.

"In obedience to the inspirations and wishes of heaven, the Roman Pontiff, the Vicar of Christ on earth, and our Father and Supreme Master, has consecrated the entire world to your Heart, O Lady. The bishops of Spain, following as always the bishop of Rome, have likewise consecrated their dioceses, and since the official life of a Catholic nation should reflect the religious life of its citizens and render worship to God according to the teaching of the Church, the Spanish State hastens today before your altar to officially consecrate the whole country to your most pure Heart, putting it under the protection of your maternal love...

"Who can enumerate the countless blessings which we owe to your protection? Accordingly then, O Mother and Mistress, filled with gratitude and love, but also with humility on account of our weaknesses, and aware of the rights which you have over us as Mother of God and as Coredemptrix and our advocate, re-affirming our Catholic, apostolic and Roman faith, and our adherence to the Vicar of Christ, and renewing our resolution to live a holy Christian life, both as individuals and as a nation... In the name of the twenty-nine million people of Spain who are united in this solemn, official and irrevocable act, we consecrate Spain to your Immaculate Heart. Regard it as your property and your possession; protect and defend it; be the sure path to lead us to God; be our mediatrix and our advocate; obtain for us from God pardon for our sins, faithfulness to the Christian law and perseverance in good. Bless our fields and our enterprises so that our people may serve you with a generous heart, free from all anxieties, since you are the Mother of us all; give us a spirit of fraternity for one another, and Christian love, for all nations and all human beings.

"Grant that through the maternal reign of your Heart, there may also come to pass for us the reign of Jesus Christ, your Son, the reign of justice and holiness, the reign of peace, love and grace. Amen."

At the end of a fine radio broadcast, in which he extolled the centuries-old devotion of Spain to the Most Holy Virgin, Pope Pius XII himself also read out an act of consecration of the nation to the Immaculate Heart of Mary, thereby associating himself with the solemn act which was carried out on the same day at Saragossa.

It was also in this period in the reign of Pius XII that the message of Fatima spread with marvellous success in the English-speaking countries.

"How can one not attribute to Our Lady of Fatima,"

reasons Canon Barthas, "the thousands upon thousands of conversions from Communism or Protestantism obtained by her great apostle in the United States, Mgr. Fulton Sheen? Especially when some of the most influential Communists, such as Douglas Hyde or Hamish Fraser, declared that they owed their return to the Catholic cradle to the intercession of Our Lady of Fatima?"

In America, to take the year 1949 alone, for example, there were no fewer than 120,000 conversions to Catholicism, and these years were also marked by the rapid development of the Blue Army of Fatima, which thenceforward was encouraged by Cardinal Tisserant. On 13 October 1954, Mgr. da Silva blessed the first stone at Fatima of the Domus Pacis, which was to become its international headquarters. Mgr. Rupp, who at that time was auxiliary bishop of Paris, supported the Blue Army in France with all his power. In 1956, its statutes were approved by the Holy See *ad experimentum*, and on 13 October of the same year, Cardinal Tisserant blessed the Domus Pacis in his capacity as papal legate. By 1959 the Blue Army numbered nearly 15 million members.

The Virgin of Fatima even seems to have given a visible sign of this marvellous power which has been granted to her for the conversion of souls. On 8 December 1952, Abbé Richard had organised a great conference on Fatima and on the Blue Army which he was about to launch in France, and which was held at Paris, in the hall of the Parc des Expositions. Mgr. Rupp gave a remarkable speech and Hamish Fraser was also due to talk. Hamish Fraser was an outspoken Scotsman who had served as a Communist commissar in the Spanish Civil War, and after his recent conversion to Catholicism he had become an ardent apostle of the message of Fatima.

Just before Fraser began his speech, a priest released a couple of doves, and at the same moment Our Lady's statue made its entrance, loudly accompanied by hymns. The doves, frightened out of their wits, flew two or three times about the hall, and then hid in the rafters. But one of them first circled around as if looking for someone and, out of the thousands of people who filled the hall, selected Hamish Fraser and calmly perched on his head, in the midst of his bushy hair; it remained there for a few minutes, apparently quite undismayed by the flashes made by the photographers, who were vying with one another in their efforts to get a shot of the scene, and then flew off to rejoin its companions.

In the course of his speech, Hamish Fraser stated: "As a result of my own personal experience, therefore, I cannot say in all honesty that I *believe* prayer can convert Communists.   I *know* that prayer can convert Communists. And because the conversion of Russia and the conversion of Communists is one and the same thing...   I *know* that prayer can convert Russia. **Whether or not Russia will be converted, whether or not there will be a third global war, whether or not the Church of Jesus Christ will return to the catacombs, depends on the answer to one question. That question is: are we prepared to pray for the conversion of Russia? Are we prepared to offer up the family Rosary every single evening in our own homes for that most worthy intention? In brief, are we prepared to do as we have been requested by the Mother of God herself? If we answer that question in the affirmative, Russia will be converted: there will be peace: we shall be able to face the future with confidence...**

"If, today, the Mystical Body of Jesus Christ is being crucified, it is not the Communists who are primarily responsible. The Stalinist soldiers who are driving the nails into Christ's Mystical Body are the agents, not of the Kremlin, but of our apathy, our lethargy, our disloyalty and our cowardice... **The moment we Catholics begin to accept our full responsibilities,**

Communism will become as irrelevant as the Arian heresy...

"In my humble opinion, Fatima is the most significant event of the century; perhaps the most significant event since the Reformation." (Hamish Fraser, *Fatal Star*, pp.223-228).

Yes, truly all the wonderful events recounted in this chapter amply justify the words applied by Pope Pius XII to the world voyage of the Pilgrim Virgin: "Heaven rained down blessings, and marvels of grace multiplied everywhere, to such an extent that we can hardly believe what our eyes are seeing".

Did not the Virgin of Fatima, by her world-wide missionary apostolate, thereby want to show the pope and the bishops with startling clarity the all-powerful nature of her intercession for the conversion of souls and the safe-guarding of nations? Was this not already the sign of her incomparable promise? Yes – as she had already amply demonstrated she could – should would convert Russia, "if my requests are heeded".

It is that simple condition – the response of the Church to her requests – which is the key to the final and yet-to-be-consummated chapter in the great drama of Fatima, through which we are living today.

At the very moment when Our Lady was working signs and wonders most powerfully throughout the world, in ratification of her promise, a movement in opposition to this divine renewal was raised up within the Church herself, to persuade the Vicar of Christ if possible to decline to proceed to the consummation of the stupendous grace proffered for the conversion of Russia. Knowing in advance the outcome of this rejection of His Will, Our Lord complained to Sister Lucia:

"Make known to My Ministers, that as they follow the example of the King of France in delaying the execution of My wishes, they will follow him into misfortune... they will repent and do it, but it will be late. Russia will already have spread her errors throughout the world, provoking wars and persecutions of the Church; the Holy Father will have much to suffer."

It is the mystery of how this opposition to Fatima from within the Church came to prevail over the better judgment of Pope Pius XII, and in the face of the radiant miracles of grace worked by the Virgin, which forms the last part of this book.

Chapter X

FATIMA ATTACKED FROM WITHIN

It may seem incredible to the reader, after the well-nigh overwhelming evidence in the preceding pages of the marvellous supernatural interventions of Our Lady of Fatima in this strife-ridden and sin-laden modern world, that anyone, let alone those in authority in our holy mother the Church, could want to discard Our Lady and her message; but that is the further uncomfortable truth which Fatima calls us to face, and the final section of this book is written to substantiate and discuss this tragic and unforeseen development.

To the critic of Fatima, there are two problems which call to be resolved. First of all, as with all other apparitions or extraordinary phenomena, there is the question of the supernatural character of the facts. As far as this is concerned, the apparitions at Fatima in 1917 are no different from those at the rue du Bac, Lourdes or Pontmain. But Fatima presents a second difficulty. Father Alonso, the great expert who was officially charged with writing the critical history of the apparitions, explains it in these words: "Without doubt, the greatest difficulty which is presented by Fatima, from the historical, critical, and literary point of view, for those who seek to study it seriously, is the progressive increase which is noticed in the facts and in the message." (J-M. Alonso, *Vraies et fausses apparitions dans l'Eglise*, p.59).

What a contrast with Lourdes, where the Virgin Mary appeared to Bernadette from 11 February to 16 July of the same year 1858. The message was already perfectly known by the end of the year. Only a few very secondary details were added later in the six written accounts which Bernadette was to draw up between 1861 and 1866. Thus at Lourdes, everything was known almost immediately, and eight years after the apparitions the seer had completely fulfilled her mission as witness.

With Fatima, everything was different! It seems that since 1917 the message has continually increased. There seems to be no end to the new apparitions or divine communications with which Lucia has continued to be favoured: in 1925 and 1926, in 1927, 1929, 1930, in 1941, 1943; and we stop at this date because there is no information thereafter.

But, more than that, from 1935 to 1941 in her *Memoirs* on the apparitions of 1917 themselves, Lucia recounts words of the Virgin and facts which she had kept secret up till that time: the two first parts of the Great Secret of 13 July 1917 were not revealed until 1942! As for the third part of the Secret, which was written down in 1943, that has still not yet been divulged. Fatima, therefore, far from being concluded, is still developing today.

It is this divergence between the initial apparitions and revelations, and their succeeding developments, which has caused confusion among some historians of Fatima, and which has served as the pretext for the most serious criticism of Fatima to be mounted from within the Church.

The most subtle, the most tenacious and certainly the most effective offensive against Fatima was led, from 1944, by a Belgian Jesuit, Father Edward Dhanis. Professor of theology at the University of Louvain from 1933 to 1949, Father Dhanis then taught at the Gregorian University at Rome, to which he was appointed rector by Pope Paul VI in 1963. With the passage of time, it can be seen today that he was the most unyielding and terrible adversary of Fatima, especially because of his apparent objectivity and his prudent moderation. His role was decisive.

It was he who opened the debate in 1944 with two long articles published in Flemish, entitled "Apropos the apparitions and the predictions of Fatima". Early in 1945, he published these two texts, very slightly recast, as a book entitled *Apropos the Apparitions and the Secret of Fatima – a Critical Contribution*. Although expressed with a thousand precautions and with great discretion, the principal thesis of his work clearly emerges: Yes, the apparitions of the Virgin to the three little shepherds of Aljustrel in 1917 are without doubt authentic; that must be conceded, because it is scarcely possible to do anything else... But as for what has been added later, all that is very much subject to caution and more than doubtful! There is nothing in that part which obliges us to believe in it, and it would be better to keep to the "first version" of the message.

His thesis received an initial reply in 1946 from the hand of a Dutch Montfortian priest, Father Jongen, who, having had the favour of an interview with Sister Lucia, was already able to make a number of interesting corrections. However it was not until 1951 that the best specialist on Fatima at that time, Father da Fonseca, who was also a Jesuit, published a point-by- point refutation of the work of his colleague, which appeared in the Portuguese review *Broteria* (May 1951, pp.505-542). Father Dhanis, who had been made a professor at the Gregorian University in 1949, then claimed that he had been misunderstood. In an article which was published in French this time, in *Nouvelle Revue Théologique* (June 1952, pp. 580-606), he tried to justify himself by accusing his colleague of having distorted his thesis.

The argument swung back against him the following year, when Father Veloso, S.J., in the same Portuguese review, contrasted the too personalised and superficial defence of Father Dhanis with the solid arguments of Father da Fonseca (*Broteria,* Feb.1953, pp.170-191).

When he was finally invited by his superiors to put an end to the scandal of a controversy which was becoming more and more bitter between members of the Society,

Father Dhanis published a confused and embarrassed article, (which appeared in the *Civilta Cattolica* for 16 May 1953, pp. 392-406), with the object, by means of a mass of prudent circumlocutions, of calming the anger of his opponents, while at the same time making it clear to his friends that he had in no way repudiated his criticisms of Fatima. For we know from a trustworthy source, a Jesuit and one of his friends who was in constant contact with him at Rome, that Father Dhanis never retracted a single one of his virulent criticisms of Fatima. - This is the man who, as we will see, enjoyed an uninterrupted series of promotions from 1960 onwards, before dying in 1978, honoured by all as one of the men in whom Pope Paul VI had had the greatest confidence.

In any event, from 1945 onwards Father Dhanis became the indispensable reference and the official source of all the adversaries of Fatima. What good fortune for them! Who could have suspected the good faith and the orthodoxy of the eminent professor at the Gregorian? Whereas the brilliant responses of the Fatima historians, published in the Portuguese review *Broteria,* were consigned to the most total oblivion, the studies of Father Dhanis created lasting repercussions in intellectual circles after the war. Numerous reviews praising his work were published far and wide. They graciously attributed to the original, which, being in Flemish, was not readily accessible to most people, all the weight of a definitive and unanswerable criticism. One article especially by Father Journet, in his review *Nova et Vetera* (May-Aug. 1948, pp. 186-188), was full of irony and violence against Fatima, and was to bring grave harm to the cause of the apparitions. The future cardinal was a fervent disciple and friend of Jacques Maritain, and also of Mgr. Montini, the future Pope Paul VI, and at that time under-secretary of State. Whence the importance of the debate for the future of the Church.

From then on, it was knowingly asserted in so-called well-informed circles that the study of Father Dhanis, the only one to possess any "scientific value", threw a legitimate suspicion over a whole part of the message. For example, Abbé René Laurentin stated in 1961: "The critical work on Fatima attempted by Father Dhanis, S.J., has aroused violent reaction... The intentions of Father Dhanis were honest, and his conclusions on the fundamental matters were reserved; as for the way in which he proceeded, he simply followed the rules governing historical criticism in any domain, even that of the Holy Scriptures. He was nevertheless regarded as having written in an ungodly spirit." In making this statement, doubtless Abbé Laurentin, like the majority of liberal and progressive Catholics opposed to Fatima, had read nothing more than the article in the *Nouvelle Revue Théologique,* and was simply echoing the opinions expressed in it: namely, that the negative conclusion of the learned Jesuit Dhanis absolves one from any obligation to make a serious and attentive examination of the documentation on Fatima.

After working on the preparation for the Council, the Belgian Jesuit was nominated consultor to the Holy Office in 1962, and rector of the Gregorian University in 1963; in 1966 he was put in charge of the Congress on "the theology of Vatican II," and in 1967 the Pope chose him as the special secretary of the first synod of bishops. The pilgrimage of Pope Paul VI to Fatima on 13 May 1967 occasioned a great wave of hostile opinion, and the authority of Father Dhanis at that time seems to have been carried to a new peak. Articles were published, citing him with almost boundless respect and admiration, by I.C.I., by Abbé Laurentin, by Fesquet writing in *Le Monde,* and by Father Rouquette writing in *Études,* from which the following extract has been taken, as an example of the tone of these articles:

"It is certainly regrettable that no serious study has been devoted to the events of Fatima, similar to that of

Louis Bassette on La Salette or of Abbé Laurentin on Lourdes... Only one critical essay has been attempted... It is the work of a theologian whose orthodoxy is *omni exceptione major*, Father Dhanis, an influential member of the theological commission of the Council, and consultor of the Roman Congregation for the Doctrine of the Faith...

"Apart from the work of Father Dhanis, the abundant literature on Fatima, which is said to be so edifying, exhibits such a poverty that it drew these indignant lines in 1948 from Cardinal Journet:

'We are told there was a 'dance' of the sun, a 'rain of flowers' and after that we are told that 'the greatest miracle', the 'miracle of miracles', is the present flourishing situation of Portugal. Just what do you take us for, gentlemen? The imprimatur can protect you from heresies, but it is powerless against stupidity. O great and mysterious Virgin of the Gospel of Christmas and of the Gospel of the Crucifixion! O great and blessed Theotokos, both redoubtable and maternal!... In these days when your faithful have more need of You than ever, will they have nothing more to inhale than these paper flowers?' " (*Les Études*, July-Aug. 1967, pp. 81, 82).

The spirit of contempt evident in these words is beyond comment. Father Rouquette quotes Cardinal Journet, who himself quotes a review by Otto Karrer of the work of Dhanis. It is always to his work that the critics of Fatima in the heart of the Church for these past thirty-five years return again and again.

In May 1982, in an article on the Secret of Fatima in the review *Historia* (pp. 44-56), Abbé Laurentin again quotes Father Dhanis as his authority. So by common consent Dhanis is the only Catholic critic who has seriously opposed Fatima, or at least the Message in all its integrity. All those who have followed him have simply gone back to his arguments as the unique source, copying and re-iterating them.

As we have said, Dhanis' two original articles were published in the *Revue Streven* (pp. 129-149, 193-215), in 1944, but there is only space here to analyse the essential elements of his thinking, since his style is to advance audacious hypotheses which completely ruin the authenticity of the apparitions, followed by long-winded and apparently reasonable passages designed to appease the reader.

All his objections are founded on the belated increase in the Message. Dhanis claims that there are in fact two histories of Fatima, the "old" one, which he calls Fatima I, and which was the version in circulation up to about 1938-40, and the "new" one, called Fatima II, which was written in the notebooks drawn up more recently by Sister Lucia between 1935 and 1941.

Such a radical distinction almost necessarily throws a grave suspicion on the unique source of Fatima II, namely, Sister Lucia's *Memoirs*. Although he concedes that Lucia's accounts "charm the reader with the innocence, piety and heroism of the privileged children" (*Streven*, p.143), nevertheless Dhanis deliberately challenges their value as historical testimony: "it is not easy to decide what credit can be given to the reports of Lucia... it might be considered prudent not to rely on her writings except with circumspection" (*Nouvelle Revue Théologique*, p.589 – henceforth abbreviated as NRT). For Dhanis believes he has uncovered serious contradictions and errors in Lucia's accounts of the events at Fatima.

He simply does not accept her explanation of the children's silence on the apparitions of the Angel in 1916. As for the theology of one of the prayers they learnt from the Angel, the censor of Fatima considers it "neither heretical nor false, but scarcely exact (mais peu exacte)". Hence, "that is sufficient to make it difficult to grant it the celestial origin which Lucia attributes to it..." (NRT, pp.590,591).

On the vision of hell, the conclusion which any

normal reader would have drawn from reading Dhanis,
as perfectly summarised by Father da Fonseca in *Fatima
e a critica* (pp.528,529), was that of "an exaggeratedly
medieval representation of the pains of hell... the critic
wonders how it came about that Our Lady could have
presented it in the 20th century." On the subject of the
famous "night illuminated by an unknown light," Dhanis
insinuated that this was not a true prophecy, since it
was not divulged until 1942 – in other words, after
the event. On the consecration of Russia, as we shall
see in more detail in chapter 12, Dhanis questions
whether "the most holy Virgin could have asked for a
consecration which, if interpreted according to the strict
meaning of the words, was practically unrealizeable?...
This question does seem to call for a negative response."
(NRT, p.595).

All these questionable accounts derive, as Dhanis is at
pains to point out, from one witness alone - Lucia. He
suggests that her testimony is uncertain because it is
unauthorized and could certainly be illusory. She might
also have "an unconscious tendency to make up fables
(une propension à la fabulation inconsciente) in a certain
sector, or at all events to recall her 20-year-old memories
with appreciable enrichments and modifications." (NRT,
p.589).

Hence, on the question of the apparition of the
Angel, Dhanis lets it be understood that Lucia imagined
them, when he says, "one may not venture to discard
absolutely the hypothesis of an account which for the
most part derives from the imagination, and one feels
moved not to adopt a definite position" (NRT, p.588;
Streven, p.209).

It is the authenticity of the Secret with which Dhanis
is really pre-occupied, as with all modern theologians.
If Lucia is making up fables, obviously the Secret loses
all its value. In order to ruin its significance
completely, Dhanis finds a subtle explanation, one
which is apparently wise and measured and devoid of all

passion. "All the same, we will not suppose that Lucia invented the whole of her account of the Secret, out of nothing, just like that". No! It is not worth it. Dhanis unceasingly asserts that he believes in the perfect sincerity of Lucia and in her good sense in daily life. Here, then, in the following passage, is the elegant solution which conciliates all, including the good faith of the seer with the inventive imagination: "We are thus led to think that, in the course of the years, certain exterior events and certain spiritual experiences of Lucia have enriched the original content of the Secret. But we also maintain that the belated writing down of the Secret is really one more echo of the mysterious words confided to the little shepherds of Fatima." (*Streven*, p. 201). "The text of the message (i.e., of the Secret) has preserved a kernel which corresponds to the words heard in 1917" but a "crust of belated elements has formed round it."

Applying this audacious reconstruction, for example, to the vision of hell, Dhanis proposes that this vision "corresponds to the idea which the children themselves had formed of hell". So did they purely and simply invent this vision? No, but instead of accepting that the vision was authentic, Dhanis suggests that "the seers received a very intense awareness of the horror of sin and damnation, and this awareness gradually evoked a vision in their imagination." (*Streven*, p. 197). In other words, the children received an inexpressibly intimate experience which they translated clumsily, following the medieval formation which they had received from the catechism. We must be intelligent, and not take their words literally.

On the theme of the Immaculate Heart of Mary, the Secret was enriched in this respect by the "infiltration of certain elements stemming from the visions of 1925-1926" at Pontevedra. Indeed, Dhanis accuses Lucia quite simply of vulgar plagiarism —although doubtless unconscious on her part, of course, as he never questions Lucia's sincerity! — when he comments on the striking

resemblance between the "great promise" which Lucia has
transmitted to us, and the "great promise" made by the
Sacred Heart to St. Margaret Mary: "thus the knowledge
of the former promise could be the psychological origin
of the new one."

Thus Dhanis' thesis, which aims above all at rejecting
the authenticity of the Secret, can be resumed under
three headings, each of which are indissolubly linked to
the other:

**1. The opposition between Fatima I and Fatima
II, as very briefly summarized above.**

2. Fatima II is the fruit of a fable.

As time went on, and up to the last article he
published on the subject in the *Civilta Cattolica* on 16
May 1953, Dhanis' attacks on Fatima became more and
more veiled, so that if you only read his last article you
would completely misunderstand his true thinking. In
order, therefore, to understand his study correctly, it is
essential to refer to his original texts of 1944-45. At no
time did he ever agree to withdraw the least line from
these fundamental texts, and it is there that his
judgement on Fatima II clearly stands out, as is shown
in the following little known but highly important
passage, taken from his general conclusion:

"The new history of Fatima, the one which is based
on the reports of Lucia, calls for more reserve. Without
denying the sane judgement and sincerity of the seer, we
should fear that certain inventions have slipped into her
narrative. The apparitions of the Angel and the
miraculous communion which he is said to have
distributed to the little seers remains uncertain. The
recently published Secret presents a rather complex
situation. Its existence has been known since 1917, and
what the children allowed of its contents to show through
very vaguely does correspond to the text which has now
been published. But several points raise real difficulties.
The description can correspond to a symbolic vision
given to the children. The messages of Our Lady

nevertheless bear the traces of different additions. Thus
it seems scarcely likely that Our Lady should have
demanded the consecration of Russia, or that she should
have attributed the provocation of the present war
exclusively to the atheist propaganda of that country.
The announcement of the aurora borealis gives rise to a
certain mistrust; and the new theme of the Immaculate
Heart of Mary does not appear in very reassuring
circumstances..." (*Streven*, p.213).

Apart from two or three prudent concessions and a
few hesitant attenuations, which are compensated for in
the earlier part of his article by contrary affirmations, if
you re-read the great Secret phrase by phrase you will see
that there remains absolutely nothing at all of the
Message of Fatima. Nothing has escaped the corrosive
criticism of Dhanis.

Is he therefore an unrelenting enemy of Fatima? He
is very anxious to avoid this accusation, especially from
the hierarchy. So he has taken care to defend himself
against it... Moreover, he considers that he has a
perfect defence against such an accusation, for does he
not profess that he accepts "all the essential part" of the
Message of Fatima? It is this which forms the third
affirmation of his thesis, namely that:

3. Fatima I remains authentic.

Fatima I, in the view of Dhanis, consists in "the facts
which have been well known from the beginning, which
appear (sic) to be confirmed as supernatural by a great
divine sign, facts to which is attached an ecclesiastical
approbation and which have become the source of a large
torrent of graces"; these are "the essential elements of the
miracle of Fatima" which he warns his reader not to
reject, "however little faith they may have in the
apparitions of the Angel (and hence in the Secret)." On
the other side, "one finds accounts which are difficult to
believe in writings which report memories as old as
twenty years... There is no sufficient reason to declare
that these facts are interdependent with the said

accounts." (*Streven,* p.148).

Is such a thesis in fact tenable?

In the light of true theology – that is to say, the supernatural knowledge which we have of God by faith – we have to say that the thesis of Father Dhanis is unthinkable, unjustifiable and even scandalous. The God who would guarantee with such miracles a seer who is unbalanced, telling fables, and unworthy of faith, has absolutely nothing in common with the true God of biblical revelation, or with Jesus, "the faithful witness" who came to bear witness to the truth, any more than with the God of Catholic dogma! For God would be lying if He worked miracles to induce the mass of the faithful, the hierarchy, and even the Pope, to believe in unworthy witnesses. For the honour of God, it would be preferable to state that all Fatima is an imposture, a vast deception plotted by priests. For whereas men can be hypocrites, self-interested and liars, God Himself never tells a lie! This vivid truth seems to have completely escaped Father Dhanis.

In the eyes of faith, the two contrary judgements on Fatima I and Fatima II are irreconcilable. We can say a priori that if all the recorded miracles are true miracles – and Dhanis himself describes them as "divine signs, authenticating the apparitions" (NRT, p.582) – then it is impossible that Lucia, the principal witness, should be so little credible. God could not have allowed her subsequently to spread throughout the Church with impunity a new history of Fatima which was radically false and which she had invented from nothing. It is impossible that a false secret, which was simply the fruit of her sickly imagination, should have deceived thousands of the faithful, with the blessing of Pope Pius XII, who had it published in 1942, and approved it many times thereafter.

If Lucia has been deceiving the world for half a century, then it is God Himself who is first of all responsible for it. For how could He have tolerated such a breach of faith on the part of the witness whom He chose, and allowed such a scandal to arise? Without ever giving His Church the slightest clear sign of the failure and treason of His messenger? After accrediting her words with miracles, would He have allowed her to deceive the whole Church — and to what a degree! — without ever giving any natural or supernatural sign to demonstrate beyond doubt that she had betrayed her function? That is impossible.

The conclusion is inescapable: in whatever way one envisages it, the thesis of Father Dhanis is untenable from the point of view of the Catholic Faith, and the ultimate proof that this is so can be found in the imposing list of disciples whom he raised up. All of them very clearly understood the meaning of his study. Abandoning without scruple the jesuitical circumlocutions of their master, they passed openly onto the attack, unduly transforming all his suspicions into solid and well-established conclusions of historical criticism. Hence, no longer embarrassed by Dhanis' prudent retention of belief in Fatima I, it was on the whole of Fatima that they brought to bear their criticisms, their insults and their sarcasms.

It is necessary to read the stupefying revision of the work of Dhanis by Cardinal Journet in his review, *Nova et Vetera*, published in the issue of May-August 1948 (pp. 186-188). It is a cantankerous indictment, full of passion and scorn for everything to do with Fatima. Nothing is neglected. All the most fragile hypotheses of Dhanis are included, one on top of the other, as so many unavoidable accusations. After reading it, there is nothing left of Fatima!

Journet was not alone in following Dhanis. In his work *Fatima y la Critica*, Father Alonso gives an impressive list of all those who have "repeated" Dhanis. They are legion; the list takes up nearly 30 pages of his book (pp. 407-435), and they come from almost every country of Europe: Otto Karrer, Schäzler,

Brennikmeyer, de Letter, Martindale, Stählin, Karl Rahner, Kloppenburg, Baumann, Bernardus. The list is not exclusive. Others have followed them: Jacquemet, Fesquet, Rouquette, and so on.

How, then, is the critic to resolve the problem posed by the fact of the apparitions and the miracles of Fatima? The accounts of the apparitions and the miracles of Fatima pose a fascinating problem for the critic. Whether the historian considers them as credible or not, these are facts of which he has to take account. The Modernist explanation is fundamentally incoherent. And what of the rationalist explanation, that it was all a piece of clerical trickery? That suggestion has absolutely no foundation, and is ridiculous and grotesque. What then is the answer?

There can only remain the solution resulting from the most serious historical criticism, which concludes in the perfect credibility of the evidence and thus in the supernatural origin of the events of Fatima.

This conclusion flows from two proofs. The first is the negative proof, which demonstrates from the facts the impossibility of maintaining any other solution, and the inconsistency of positing any "natural explanation". The counterpart of this is the second, positive proof, which directly establishes the credibility of the witnesses. There is such a weight of material that both these arguments could be developed almost indefinitely. Let us focus on just one fact which by itself is the rock which guarantees the authenticity of Fatima. One of the best Fatima historians, the Portuguese Costa Brochado, explains it very clearly in his book *Fatima a Luz da Historia* (p.216): "When we regard them in the light of history, the events of Fatima do not depend on the three seers. It is not they who have given these events their historical character, but the indisputable evidence of thousands of people. The astonishing solar phenomena of 13 October 1917, which we are going to study, are historical realities which even the seers themselves could not contradict today, if by chance they were to rise from their tombs to claim that they saw nothing." And this extraordinary historical event has only one explanation: it is the divine miracle sent to confirm the authenticity of the apparitions which, three months before, had announced the event to the day and the hour. That is a fact which even Father Dhanis himself, despite all his prejudices, is obliged to admit in company with all the Fatima historians. The prodigious solar phenomenon of 13 October 1917 is indeed the miraculous foundation and the major event on which is based our faith in the supernatural origin of the apparitions of 1917. The miracle of the sun is to the events and to the message of Fatima, what the miracle of the Resurrection of Christ is to the Gospel: the solid basis of the whole structure, and the certain, objective, historical fact which guarantees by its necessarily divine origin the authenticity of the revelation to which it is indissolubly linked.

The long history of Marian apparitions for more than a century serves to illustrate the prudent wisdom of the Church, who knows how to discern with certitude the authentic divine manifestations, recognising and distinguishing them from all their fraudulent pathological or diabolical imitations, which she unmasks and denounces.

Supported by the facts brought out by a rigorous process of historical criticism, the Church gave her pronouncement upon Fatima with firmness and authority. Following the official recognition by the Bishop of Leiria in 1930, Fatima has enjoyed the constant and unanimous approval of the popes and of the bishops of the whole world, even though many of them have taken their time to comply with Our Lady's requests.

The following statement of Cardinal Cerejeira, the patriarch of Lisbon, at Rome on 11 February 1967, perfectly expressed the judgment of the Catholic hierarchy on the events of Fatima: "No, Fatima is not the ecclesiastical exploitation of superstitious ignorance; Fatima is a source of light and grace which the Immaculate Virgin caused to spring up in the heart of Portugal...

"It is not the Church which has imposed Fatima (on the faithful), it is Fatima which has imposed itself on the Church... Despite the reserve of the Church and the obstinate and ridiculous opposition of the State, Fatima continued to touch the religious conscience of the country. Without the help of the Church and against the power of the State, the light of the miracle radiated with ever-increasing brilliance throughout Portugal, and the warmth of the enthusiasm of the people spread throughout the whole country.

"...Fatima compels recognition by the evidence of a supernatural action which, I have no hesitation in affirming, is scarcely without parallel in the history of Marian interventions... In our times of atheistic materialism, Fatima shows us in a startling manner that the supernatural world exists. Fatima proves it to us in a visible, tangible, unchallengeable and even flagrant manner. Fatima annihilates the absurd and arbitrary negation of the supernatural, formulated in the name of reason and science..." (Documentation Catholique, 19 March 1967, col. 546-547,550).

This brilliant light, which radiates from the apparitions of 1917, guarantees the authenticity of the whole message of Fatima. What a foreboding omen for the Church, then, that just at the time when Pope Pius XII declared to the leaders of the Blue Army, on 8 May 1950: "...the time for doubting Fatima is past, it is now time for action...", Father Dhanis, pointing in exactly the opposite direction to that already indicated by the Church herself and the Holy Father, was hard at work organising a campaign of criticism directed against Fatima.

It is not the object of this study to make a detailed

refutation of the criticisms of Father Dhanis, which can be found in chapters one and three of my book, *La Science et Les Faits*, which is volume I of my three-volume study, *Toute la Verite Sur Fatima*, and from which the passages in this present volume have been selected and translated. Suffice it to say in summary of the evidence which I demonstrate from his own writings, that the thesis of Father Dhanis is quite untenable owing to the incoherence of his theological argument and his method of criticism. But it is equally inadmissible because it is false in its own principle, being based on an entirely erroneous affirmation as well as being propped up by quite valueless objections.

The whole critical fabric of Father Dhanis' work is based on the supposed distinction between the "former history" of Fatima as circulated up to the years 1938 to 1940, and the "new history" which has been increased since that period by the contribution of Sister Lucia's memoirs. These two histories were described by Father Dhanis as Fatima I and Fatima II (*Nouvelle Revue Théologique*, 1952, p. 598). While it is undeniable that there has been a progressive growth in the diffusion of the message, Dhanis has concluded from that fact that this has produced a real, objective division.

In his work, Father Dhanis practically ignores a distinction of the greatest importance. When analysing the transmission of the message of Fatima, just as with any historical data, four successive stages can be distinguished:

    1. First of all, there is the event itself and the first oral evidence reporting it: in this case, the replies of the children to the interrogations in 1917.

    2. Then there is the subsequent oral evidence, which cannot be neglected. Dhanis ignores this evidence completely.

    3. Then comes the writing down of the event. The writings of Sister Lucia, principally accounts and letters to her confessors, are much more numerous than imagined by Father Dhanis. Although they remained unpublished for a long time, as a means of putting a date to the alleged appearance of a new theme in the message they are unquestionably sound historical documents. Dhanis does not take them into account.

4. **Finally there comes the moment of divulgation.** In the case of Fatima, it was often very belated, against the will of the seer herself, and purely owing to the wishes of the ecclesiastical authorities. The divulgation of the Secret and of several other themes essential to the message was not to take place until 1942, and the last part of the Secret has still not been revealed.

Dhanis constructs his whole system by only taking account of the two extremes, ignoring the intermediate stages altogether! To the formal evidence of 1917 he wantonly opposes the popular accounts of the event published in the 1940s, and roundly concludes that in between is a highly suspect process of continuity which can only be explained by the belated invention of all the new themes! But when one examines the whole sequence of intermediate evidence between the interrogations of 1917 and the divulgation of 1942, the alleged lack of continuity disappears. Accordingly, the whole hypothesis of Father Dhanis falls to the ground.

Those studies of Father Alonso which have been published to date, while waiting for the release of his monumental critical work of 14 volumes, which the Bishop of Leiria officially commissioned him to undertake, already make it clear that there was an uninterrupted chain of oral or written testimonies, which indicate that Lucia already knew and had partly revealed everything which she was accused of having invented later! Even the most excessively elaborate historical criticism is thus able to establish that the seers did indeed receive a secret in 1917, that they kept it painstakingly, and then revealed it little by little, according to the designs of providence, as the theologians would say. In the light of all that we now know about Fatima, it is not difficult to reconstruct a chronological sequence of this progressive emergence and revelation of the Secret, showing that there is indeed complete continuity between the reception of the Secret by the seers in 1917 and its eventual publication in 1942.

1915. Contrary to the unjustified assertions of Father Dhanis, the first manifestations of an Angel were known immediately, as Lucia's little companions could not keep quiet about it when they returned to the village. Canon Formigao was told of this in 1917.

1917. In September/October, Lucia spoke of the apparitions of the Angel in 1916 to Canon Formigao, who reported it to Canon Barthas. Furthermore, as Barthas records in his book, the parents of the seers knew that, from the time of the apparitions, the little seers were accustomed to reciting certain words which they called "the prayer of the Angel", but they did not know who had taught it to them.

1920. During her illness, Jacinta revealed many secrets, especially to Mother Godinho, in which several of the themes of the Secret were already foreshadowed: the prophecy of wars and chastisements, the searing thought of Hell, the necessity for reparation. "We have documents drawn up not long after the death of Jacinta", records Alonso on page 85 of his *Histoire ancienne et histoire nouvelle*.

1921-1922. A serious enquiry by Canon S.dos Reis, which was separately confirmed by Father Alonso, established that from this period Lucia taught the prayers of the Angel to one of her companions of the Asilo de Vilar. These prayers already contain a reference to the Immaculate Heart of Mary. The bishop of Leiria also confirmed to Canon Barthas that Lucia had told him about the apparitions of the Angel around this time.

1924. Lucia's interrogation for the canonical process clearly brought out the existence of a secret which had not yet been revealed.

1925-1929. There are numerous documents which prove that, as from this period at least, Lucia was already in possession of the whole of "Fatima II". The alleged hiatus is thus greatly reduced. Furthermore, from this moment onwards the responsibility for its divulgation now rested entirely with the authorities to whom Lucia was bound by religious obedience. This decision was no longer hers.

1925-1926. Lucia wrote several letters to her confessors describing the apparition of the Immaculate Heart of Mary at Pontevedra, with the request for the communion of reparation of the five first Saturdays, which is already an essential part of the Secret.

1927. Lucia now received permission from Heaven to reveal the first two parts of the Secret, which she copied out twice for her confessors. This is a fact of capital importance! The first two parts of the Secret were already written down in 1927. Even though her confessors ordered her to burn the text almost immediately afterwards, the fact is no less certain for all that.

In 1946, Lucia informed Father Jongen, for the benefit of Father Dhanis, that he could write to the two confessors in question – Fathers José da Silva Aparicio and José Bernardo Goncalves - to verify the facts for himself, and that she had also revealed the Secret before the Second World War to her Provincial, to the Bishop of Leiria, and to Canon Galamba.

Father Dhanis took great care not to verify this evidence, although both men were alive at the time, and Jesuits like himself.

1929-1936. Very many documents report the apparitions of Tuy and Pontevedra, which constitute the essential part of Fatima II and its close connection with the Secret.

1935. In her first Memoir, Lucia already alludes to the passages in the Secret concerning the Immaculate Heart of Mary.

1937. The Bishop of Leiria , on behalf of Lucia,

writes to Pope Pius XI, requesting the consecration of Russia to the Immaculate Heart of Mary. Sister Lucia draws up her seond Memoir, in which she describes the apparitions of the Angel and speaks of the Immaculate Heart of Mary.

1938-1939. Sister Lucia writes several letters to her bishop announcing the imminent outbreak of the war prophesied in the Secret and already predicting that Portugal would be spared.

1940. Sister Lucia writes to Pope Pius XII. In her letter she communicates the Secret to him and describes the complementary apparitions of Tuy and Pontevedra in 1925 and 1929.

1941. Sister Lucia draws up her third and fourth Memoirs, which constitute the whole of Fatima II.

1942. It was only at this date the authorities finally permitted the Secret to be divulged, and the new themes were thus exposed in their entirety for the first time in the works of Fathers Galamba, da Fonseca and Moresco. Moreover, when Father Dhanis claims that he is scandalised by the substantial augmentation of the Message, he is overlooking a fact which he knows but to which he pays practically no attention: that **the existence of the Secret** was in truth divulged immediately, in July 1917. So Lucia could not have invented it all at a later date.

The existence of this Secret was something to which the children bore witness almost continually thereafter, and it was in fact one of the causes of the rapid success of Fatima. Everyone wanted to question the seers in order to make them reveal this famous secret, subjecting them to all sorts of tempting or frightening inducements to this end. We should not forget that it was to preserve this secret that the three children, aged ten, nine and seven, kept the most complete silence, preferring to die in a vat of boiling oil rather than disobey Our Lady, when they were imprisoned by the Administrator of Ourem. "I fully expected to be boiled alive", Sister

Lucia told John Haffert years later. There were also
other indications, apart from the secret itself, that the
seers had not yet given a complete account of the
apparitions, as the parents of Jacinta and Francisco were
only too well aware. Not without regret, their mother,
Ti Olimpia, observed: "I do not know what has got into
these children. When they are alone, they chatter like
magpies, but as soon as someone approaches they become
silent, and it is impossible to get a word out of them."
(Canon Barthas, *Fatima, Merveille du XXe siécle*, p.41).

We see, then, that we are a very long way from the
total silence between 1917 and 1942, dreamed up by
Dhanis in order to bolster up his thesis, and whose
objective above all is to reject the authenticity of the
Secret. "Confronted with this chronological table,"
concludes Father Alonso, "all the hypotheses imagined
by the negative critic of Fatima collapse. The
unfavourable judgements based on excessively late dates
are seen to be without critical foundation. The
chronological difficulty disappears of its own accord. It
is no longer a question of themes which are said to have
been completely ignored until Sister Lucia drew up her
Memoirs. It is a question of themes which belong to the
Message of Fatima and which, little by little,
providentially come out into the open." (Father Alonso,
Histoire ancienne et histoire nouvelle de Fatima, p.87).

Accordingly, the Secret which was eventually
divulged to the world in 1942 does indeed originate in
1917.

From 1944 to 1982, whether from charity or weakness,
most of the authors who referred to the works of Father
Dhanis, either to quote him as their authority or to
criticise him steadfastly, felt themselves obliged at least
to render homage to his perfect good faith. Father da
Fonseca and Father Alonso were among this number, as
well as Abbé Laurentin, who wrote, for example, in
May 1982: "Dhanis had in no way written out of
hostility against Fatima, he assured me before his death,

but because he was anxious that the doubts and inexplicable confusions, which he could perceive but not resolve, should be dissipated." (*Historia*, May 1982, p.46).

However, a rapid survey of the controversy obliges one to state that this affirmation does not correspond with the reality. Facts are facts, and for the honour of Fatima they should not be hidden. If we insist on this point, it is because the flagrant bad faith of the first and only adversary of Fatima itself renders an ultimate witness in favour of the message which he combated for reasons other than the sole love of the truth, and by arms other than that of an objective scientific criticism, without prejudice or passion.

We certainly recognise that Dhanis' first studies, which appeared in 1944 and 1945, had at least the merit of stating with all openness and clarity the nature of the specific problem posed by Fatima for the critic, namely, the progressive growth of the message. He was likewise justly entitled to be astonished and even scandalised at the considerable retouching of the text of the great Secret by the authors who were the first to publish it. This disfigured text, which was presented by various persons in versions which differed notably among themselves, by that very fact had lost a good part of its credibility. The Belgian Jesuit had a further excuse, which he was to invoke later: "The war which was raging at the time we were writing, if it caused a few difficulties, nevertheless sharpened our minds to carry out an attentive work, driven only by the desire to honour the Most Holy Virgin by bringing to light the truth on the subject of these apparitions. However, unfortunately we were not able to consult personally the archives of the diocese of Leiria, but we were able to take stock of all the important works which appeared at that time on Fatima..." (*Civilta Cattolica*, 16 May 1953, p.403).

Notwithstanding this, is it not a matter for astonishment that a professor of Louvain, who was perfectly aware of the inadequacy of his sources – by his own avowal his study was based on popular works which were much more preoccupied with devotion than with scientific criticism – nevertheless attempted to sustain a thesis so contrary to that of his colleagues, and especially that of Father da Fonseca? All the more so since he knew that Father da Fonseca, a Jesuit like himself, and an eminent professor at the Biblical Institute, possessed the sources and the documents to which he, Dhanis, had not had access.

But it was above all in the following years that Father Dhanis behaved in a curious manner for a man who, in his own words, was only animated by love of the Most Holy Virgin and the desire to bring to light the truth about the apparitions. In 1946, Father Jongen, a Dutch Montfortian priest, sent to Sister Lucia the objections of Father Dhanis. All the replies of the seer were of a perfect clarity and precision, and above all, she offered the Fatima critic an easy means of verifying all that she had said, by giving him the names of all the persons to whom she had revealed, from 1927 to 1941, the contents of the great Secret. She told him that he could write to her confessors, to ask them what she had told them in 1927, and she also took the trouble to give him their addresses in 1946, as well as indicating the name of her superiors to whom she had revealed the same confidences. Father Jongen immediately published an account of this exchange in several Belgian reviews, and Dhanis must certainly have been aware of that. But he never made any allusion to it thereafter, which proves, either that he did not deign to write to any of these witnesses, who alone could throw a decisive light on the whole question, or that whatever he may have obtained from them was completely contrary to his own thesis. In any event, all this raises a serious suspicion about his perfect good faith.

Even more grave, it is known that the Bishop of Leiria invited him to come to Fatima to study the facts and the documents preserved in the archives, but he always refused to do so. Dom Jean-Nesmy says that "Father Dhanis never wanted to come and study the documents on the spot, nor to question Sister Lucia herself at Coimbra. Thus he did not have to deny his hypothesis, which a deeper historical inquiry would have shown him was unjustified." (*La Vérité de Fatima*, p.246, note 11). What a strange attitude! Apparently his sole desire during the war was to bring the truth to light; now that he was offered the opportunity to verify it on the spot after the war, he did not seem to want to know it. His mind was made up in advance, and in order not to have to retract his position he preferred not even to attempt to look for the facts. So when the defenders of Fatima demonstrated his errors with compelling reasons, he slipped away and fled the discussion.

Before we go on to see precisely what Dhanis did next, let us take the remarkable case of one of his disciples, Canon Journet. In 1948 he published a spiteful article in his review *Nova et Vetera*, full of glaring errors and slanderous remarks directed against the seer and some of the Fatima historians, notably Canon Barthas. Moreover the article had practically no critical value whatever. But when Canon Barthas demanded a correction, he refused to allow it.

To return to Father Dhanis. When in June 1952 he sought to reply to the masterly refutation of his thesis by Father da Fonseca – a refutation which was both benevolent, demonstrative and rich in new documents – he resorted to the same less than honourable procedure, adding to his text this revealing note, which was attributed to the editor of the review: "Our collaborator shows that his thought has been distorted in the study which was devoted to it (by Father da Fonseca). The *Nouvelle Revue Théologique* is of the opinion that it is making an equitable gesture in the service of the truth by publishing this reply (of Father Dhanis); it considers that the debate is now closed." So Father da Fonseca was not allowed to reply.

Confronted with the arguments and the previously unpublished documents brought out by the Fatima specialist, Father Dhanis side-stepped and refused all discussion on the fundamental questions. He declared straight away: "We have no intention of discussing this question here, which in our opinion is rather difficult to grasp." What question? Precisely the incoherence of Father Dhanis' thesis, as demonstrated by his colleague. Elsewhere, he noted in passing: "The new evidence brought forward by Father da Fonseca on the subject of the solar prodigy is interesting, but its examination does not enter into the scope of this article." Dhanis used the same evasive remark on several other occasions. In short, everything which obliged him to recognise his errors in black and white was cleverly pushed aside, on the pretext that it did not enter into the scope of his article!

But, what is even more grave, during this time he allowed all those who quoted only him as their authority to cover the seer, the apparitions and the message of Fatima with scorn, insults and slander, without ever making the slightest attempt to repudiate his extremist disciples. The latter, who after all were only expressing clearly what he himself had skilfully insinuated, claimed that they had totally ruined the evidence of Sister Lucia and drew up foolish objections against the message of Fatima, but never once did the master who had launched the offensive and furnished all the ammunition, think of making any reparation whatever to those who had been so gravely damaged by these attacks. He confined himself – and with what jealous care! – to defending his own reputation which had been compromised, waiting until the time would come, as it did after 1960, when his theories could finally be published with impunity in broad daylight and succeed in influencing the decisions of the highest authorities in the Church.

Dom Jean-Nesmy is therefore quite correct in stating that "Father Dhanis has done a great deal of harm to Fatima... But indirectly he provoked the historical research which on the contrary has confirmed the veracity of Lucia." (op.cit., p.246).

In fact, without the underhand attacks of Dhanis, would the Bishop of Fatima have thought of entrusting Father Alonso with the task of preparing a great critical study in which there should be published the entire body of the documents of Fatima, with all the necessary scientific credentials? If the final result of this monumental work has not yet been published, all the lesser publications which have been taken from it, and which surely constitute its essence, permit us to establish even now the whole truth of the entire story of Fatima with greater certainty than ever.

Chapter XI

THE CLIMAX OF THE HOLY YEAR, 1950

The progressive intelligentsia, who bitterly deplored the growing faith which the Pope appeared to place in the apparitions and the Message of Fatima, found in the critical works of Father Dhanis an effective instrument of propaganda. Mgr. Journet, the future Cardinal and friend of Mgr. Montini, referred to them in 1948 when he wrote the extremely violent article against Fatima to which we have referred above, filled with flagrant errors and lacking in any critical value, while a condensed version of the thesis of Father Dhanis was circulated among the bishops.

It does seem astonishing, given this scenario, that Father Dhanis should have been promoted professor of the Gregorian University in Rome precisely in 1949. This advance must certainly have been due to the influence of protectors, and there is every reason to believe that Father Janssens, who had been elected Superior-General of the Jesuits on 15 September 1946, and who was himself Belgian and a former professor and rector of the theological college of Louvain, had a high opinion of Father Dhanis, and had indeed decided to support him in his offensive against Fatima. However that may be, it is a fact that the glacial silence of the General of the Jesuits on the subject of Fatima makes an astonishing contrast with the enthusiastic attitude of Father Suarez, who was elected Master-General of the Dominicans in 1946.

However, the Pope reacted vigorously to the campaign against Fatima within the Church. On 12 October 1952, Father Suarez, the Master-General of the Dominicans, declared publicly at Fatima:

"If someone tells you that the Sovereign Pontiff has been deluded by Fatima, you should know that it is not true. Not long ago, while visiting our houses in central Europe during the Holy Year of 1950, I heard it said in several places that this was the confidential opinion of the Pope. On my return, I asked for a special audience and I told the Holy Father what I had heard people saying. To which the Sovereign Pontiff replied: 'I have never said or thought such a thing! What new proof do you want the Pope to give you of his love for Fatima?' 'Can I tell that to my religious?' **'Tell them that the thinking of the Pope is contained in the message of Fatima.** Tell your religious that they should continue to work with the greatest enthusiasm for the propagation of the cult of Our Lady of the Rosary of Fatima'" *(Bote von Fatima*, 10 May 1950).

Strengthened by this encouragement, Father Suarez immediately decided to install the Dominicans at Fatima. On 12 October 1951 he blessed the first stone of the convent, and on 12 October 1952 he returned to the Cova da Iria to open the new house, which was to become the noviciate and the house of studies of the Dominican province in Portugal. On that occasion Father Suarez declared: "We will stay at Fatima to propagate the Rosary as long as Our Lady wishes. Dominicans throng here from all sides, and they will leave to carry thoughout the entire world devotion to Our Lady of Fatima!"

This enthusiasm underlines, by contrast, the extreme reserve of the superiors of the Society of Jesus. Having said that, however, we do not forget the decisive role of the Portuguese Jesuits in the service of the apparitions and of the message of Fatima. We have seen the very important role played by Fathers Aparicio and Goncalves in their relations with the seer; there was also Father Morain at the side of Mgr. da Silva and Father da Fonseca at Rome, to whom Pope Pius XII had recourse for his services on several occasions. Finally, for the last fifteen years Father Antonio Maria Martins has been issuing numerous works containing hitherto unpublished documents, which have happily contributed to re-awaken interest in the history of Fatima.

It is certain that Pius XII, at the opening of the Holy Year in 1950, did not intend to be sparing in his encouragement to the apostles of Fatima. Quite the contrary. The Blue Army of Mgr. Colgan already numbered one million members, and it had just launched the publication of its magazine *Soul*. On 8th May, Mgr. Colgan was received by Pius XII in a private audience. The Pope, who had the first issues of the magazine on his desk, declared to the founder of the Blue Army:

"As world leader against Communism, I willingly give my blessing to you and to all the members of the Blue Army ... **Now the time for doubting Fatima has passed, the moment for action has come.**" (M. Dias Coelho, *Exercito Azul de Nossa Senhora de Fatima*, pp. 15-16).

However, on the question of the precise wishes of the Virgin of Fatima, in this Holy Year the Pope still seemed to hesitate to take a further step forward. It is true that Fatima and its message is mentioned a few times in the papal discourses for 1950, but they are simply allusions without much depth, and it is difficult to avoid the conclusion that the Jesuit campaign against Fatima affected the Pope all the same. At least it can be said to have done so in this sense, that he knew that any further decisions too openly favourable to Fatima would stir up a backlash and fierce opposition, and that several persons, even among his most immediate entourage, would take an unfavourable view of these initiatives. So Pius XII remained undecided.

It would seem, at this decisive hour when suddenly everything was in a state of suspension, waiting for the decision of the Sovereign Pontiff, that heaven intervened in order to enlighten and encourage the supreme Pastor of the Church to act with strength and determination in order to correspond fully to the great designs of mercy of the Sacred Hearts of Jesus and Mary. Sister Lucia had long held a lively hope of this heavenly intervention, and implored it on many occasions. Writing to Father Goncalves on 18 May 1936, she told him how already at that time she used to say in her prayers: "But, O my God, the Holy Father will not believe me if You do not move him Yourself by a special inspiration", to which Our Lord answered: "**The Holy Father! Pray much for the Holy Father. He will do it, but it will be late!**".

On 18 August 1940, Sister Lucia wrote again to Father Goncalves, and told him, on the question of the consecration of Russia by the Pope: "Our good God could, by means of some prodigy, clearly show (the Pope) that this demand comes from Him, but He is using this delay to exercise His justice, by punishing the world for so many crimes and by preparing it for a more complete return to Him". And again, in a letter published in Father A. Martins' book *Fatima e O Coracao de Maria*, she described how, in a communication on the night of 5 March 1942, Our Lord "seemed to make me more keenly aware that **He was refusing to grant peace because of the crimes which continued to provoke His justice, and also because He is not obeyed in His requests**, especially for the consecration to the Immaculate Heart of Mary, although He moved the heart of His Holiness to accomplish it."

In the autumn of 1950, the hour of mercy struck once again. On 29 October 1950, the statue of the Pilgrim Virgin of Fatima, which had just visited several nations in Asia, arrived in Rome. The following day, 35 cardinals and more than 450 bishops held a meeting in consistory at which, for the first time, the Sovereign Pontiff officially informed them of his intention to define the dogma of the Assumption in the near future. At the end of his allocution, for the last time he questioned the successors of the Apostles: "Is it your pleasure, then, venerable brethren, that we should solemnly proclaim and define as a dogma revealed by God, the bodily Assumption of the Blessed Virgin Mary into heaven?" The question met with their unanimous assent.

It was on precisely this Monday 30 October, the day after this solemn decision had been taken, and while the statue of Our Lady of Fatima remained for three days in the church of the Casaletto, just behind the Vatican gardens, on ground belonging to the Holy See, and on the anniversary day of the consecration of the world to the Immaculate Heart of Mary eight years earlier, that it was given to the Holy Father to contemplate the same extraordinary spectacle which the 70,000 pilgrims saw at the Cova da Iria on 13 October 1917. Let us hear Pius XII himself describe what happened, in an account which was written down not long afterwards, and which, according to Father da Fonseca, the Pope wrote out in his own hand for Cardinal Tedeschini:

"It was 30th October 1950, two days before the solemn definition of the Assumption into heaven of the Most Holy Virgin Mary, a day for which the whole Catholic world was waiting with such impatience. Towards 4 o'clock in the afternoon, I was taking my customary walk in the Vatican gardens, reading and studying various business papers as usual. I was walking up the esplanade of Our Lady of Lourdes towards the top of the slope, along the path to the right which skirts the surrounding wall.

"At a certain moment, having lifted my eyes above the papers which I was holding in my hand, I was struck by a phenomenon which I had never seen before. The sun, which was still fairly high, was displayed like a pale yellow opaque globe, completely surrounded by a luminous halo which, however, did not hinder one in any way from looking attentively at the sun, without feeling the slightest discomfort. There was a very light cloud in front of it.

"The opaque globe was moving towards the exterior, turning slowly upon itself, and shifting from left to right and vice versa. But very strong movements could be seen in the interior of the globe with complete clarity and without interruption. The same phenomenon took place again the next day, 31st October...". (Article by Cardinal Tedeschini in *Attualita di Fatima*, Rome 1954, pp. 76-79).

On the vigil of All Saints, which was also the vigil of the day so long awaited, a big procession of people carried in triumph the venerable image of Our Lady, Salus populi Romani, from the Ara Coeli Basilica to Saint Peter's Square.

Sister Pascalina records in her Memoirs that the Holy Father had described the superb spectacle which he had just seen, immediately on returning from his walk on 30th October. Her account is almost identical to the one we have just read above, but she adds this very interesting piece, which the former does not contain:

"The following day was a Sunday. (As we have seen, in fact the 31st October was a Tuesday. Doubtless the Sister was mistaken owing to the great solemnity of the occasion). Full of hope, we also went into the gardens, expecting that we too would be able to see the spectacle, but we had to return disappointed. The Holy Father immediately asked us: 'Did you see it? Today it was exactly like yesterday!'" (Sister M. Pascalina Lehnert, *Ich durfte ihm dienen*, pp. 154-155).

The next day, 1st November, in the course of an imposing ceremony in Saint Peter's, in the presence of between 600,000 to 700,000 pilgrims gathered round the basilica, the Pope read out the infallible words of the dogmatic definition: "We proclaim, declare and define it to be a dogma revealed by God that the Immaculate Mother of God, Mary ever Virgin, when the course of her earthly life was finished, was taken up body and soul into the glory of heaven" (*Munificentissimus Deus*, No.

53).

Let us return to Sister Pascalina's account of the day:

"A deep blue sky stood out above the cupola of Saint Peter's. **The crescent of the moon could also be seen beside the sun, just above the cross on the cupola! How was it possible? The people saw it and were amazed.** In the words of Prime of that day, 'Quae est ista... pulchra ut luna, electa ut sol'. Coming on a day which was already so remarkably warm and clear, the vision of the crescent moon above Michelangelo's cupola, at this special hour of rejoicing, created a marvellously symbolic effect" (Ibid., p.157).

After the Sovereign Pontiff had given solemn benediction to the crowd, the ceremony continued in the basilica of Saint Peter's with the singing of None and the pontifical High Mass, in which was chanted, for the first time, the admirable office which opens with the words of the seer of Patmos: "Signum Magnum apparuit in coelo, mulier amicta sole et luna sub pedibus eius... A great sign appeared in the heavens, a Woman, clothed with the sun, and the moon under her feet..." (Apoc. 12:1).

In the afternoon of this memorable day, which, as Sister Pascalina remarks, was "the crowning event and zenith of the Holy Year", and indeed of all Pius XII's pontificate, the Holy Father again took his customary walk in the Vatican gardens. Let us hear how he recorded his vision of the dance of the sun, as quoted by Cardinal Tedeschini:

"The same phenomenon took place again the following day, 31st October, and on 1st November, the day of the definition, and then again on 8th November, the octave day of the same solemnity. Since then, there has been nothing.

"On several occasions, on other days at the same time and in identical or nearly similar atmospheric conditions, I attempted to look at the sun to see if the same phenomenon was visible to my eyes, but in vain; I could not look at the sun for even a second, as my sight was immediately dazzled. That, briefly and simply, is the pure truth" (Quoted in Canon Barthas, *Fatima 1917-1968*, pp. 160-162). Sr. Pascalina describes what happened in the following words:

"The Holy Father saw (the prodigy) again on the day of the proclamation of the dogma, and once more on the octave of the feast. We would very much like to have seen it ourselves, but that was not granted to us... Pius XII had enquiries made at the Specula (in charge of the Vatican Observatory), but they knew nothing about it either and had not seen anything. Further enquiries outside the Vatican, at the request of the Holy Father, likewise produced no results" (Op.cit., p.155).

Thus Pius XII was the unique witness of this prodigy. That is why it cannot be considered as an indisputable historical fact, unlike the solar miracle of 13 October 1917, which was unanimously recognised by more than 70,000 pilgrims and people of differing convictions. The prodigy witnessed by Pius XII is of another order. However, our conviction that the facts are authentic is reinforced both by the intrinsic strength of the evidence and by the august quality of the witness.

For how could anyone – and all the more so if one is a Catholic – cast doubt on such an attestation, coming from the lips of the Holy Father himself, with such precision, such assurance and such solemnity? We are convinced, therefore, that on four separate occasions, Pope Pius XII saw a marvellous phenomenon which renewed in his eyes the miracle of the Cova da Iria. Accordingly one is led to ask: what was the meaning and the full implication of this authentic intervention by heaven in the life of the Sovereign Pontiff?

First of all, it is undeniable, as Cardinal Tedeschini was to say, doubtless echoing the confidences of the Holy Father, that this marvellous vision was "a reward" for the Pope, "a sign showing that the definition of the dogma of the Assumption had been supremely pleasing to God". The coincidence of this extraordinary phenomenon with the infallible proclamation of the dogma very clearly underlined it. For in fact the Pope had contemplated the dance of the sun on 30th October, the day when the definition was offically announced, on 31st October and on 1st November, on the vigil and the day itself of the proclamation, and finally on 8th November, the octave day of the solemnity.

It is worth recalling that on 8th December 1854, at the definition of the dogma of the Immaculate Conception by Pope Pius IX, the Sovereign Pontiff had experienced a similar manifestation from heaven. At the moment when he pronounced the infallible words, Pius IX felt that his voice was suddenly and mysteriously strengthened and amplified, to the extent that it rang throughout the whole basilica. At the same instant, whereas up to then it had been raining heavily, "precisely at the moment when the Pontiff pronounced the words of the definition, the heavens opened and a ray of light illuminated the Pontiff".

And can it not be said that the apparitions at Lourdes themselves were the divine recompense granted by the Immaculate Virgin to the Church in response to her glorification by the Sovereign Pontiff? St. Bernadette understood it in this sense, and wrote to Pope Pius IX: "How good the Virgin is! One could say that she came to confirm the words of our Holy Father."

Was not the vision of the dance of the sun a similar heavenly confirmation to Pius XII for the dogma of the Assumption? No doubt that thought was in his mind when he used an expression similar to that of the seer of Lourdes in his encyclical *Fulgens corona*: "It seems that by this prodigy the Blessed Virgin wanted to give some sort of confirmation to the sentence which the vicar of her divine Son had pronounced."

But apart from being a heavenly confirmation of the dogma of the Assumption, the vision of the dance of the sun was also invested with a more precise and more urgent significance. It was the miracle of 1917 which had been renewed, thirty-three years later, in the eyes of the Holy Father, at the Vatican. **This grace, Cardinal Tedeschini was to say again, was "a heavenly sign destined to authenticate the connection between the marvels of Fatima and the centre, the head of the Truth and of the Catholic Magisterium"**. Yes, it was the Virgin of Fatima who, doubtless in response to the humble supplications of her messenger, was giving the Sovereign Pontiff a direct and brilliant proof of the reality of the apparitions and the urgency of her message. "The time for doubting Fatima is passed. The moment for action has come", the Pope had declared a few months before. Well! the Virgin of Fatima came to encourage him to march forward resolutely along this path. The sign which she gave him was the most pressing invitation to give his assent to her message, without any further reserve or hesitation. It was also a very clear indication that the moment had come when at last all her requests should be accomplished.

Finally, this dance of the sun, which demonstrated the all-powerful mediation of the Virgin, "pulchra ut luna, electa ut sol, terribilis ut castrorum acies ordinata — beautiful as the moon, glorious as the sun, formidable like an army in battle array", was doubtless meant to signify for the Holy Father the promise of the very special protection and extraordinary help of the Queen of Heaven in all his struggles. It was the pledge of victory. After the publication of the encylical *Humani Generis* against all the modern errors, after the firm decision taken by the Pope to conclude the process of canonization of Pope Pius X despite all the opposition, and after the solemn exercise of his infallibility in the proclamation of the dogma of the Assumption, did not heaven want to encourage the Pope to continue in this direction, without further fears of any person or thing?

Yes, this brilliant sign which appeared in heaven was both the most generous recompense, the most pressing encouragement and the most marvellous promise, like

the announcement of final victory. Unhappily, Pius XII
did nothing. He preferred to wait. On 23rd November
and on 10th December, he made two brief allusions to
Fatima, and that was all.

In his Christmas 1950 broadcast, Pius XII announced
to the world that, in conformity with tradition, the
privileges of the Holy Year Jubilee would be extended to
the whole world throughout 1951. On 13 May 1951,
the news was received in Portugal, with the greatest
enthusiasm, that the Holy Father had also decided that
the solemn closure of this Holy Year "extra Urbem"
would take place on the following 13th October at the
Cova da Iria, and that it would be preceded by an
international Catholic congress on the Message of
Fatima. The congress was to last three days, and in
three public sessions it would discuss the Message of
Fatima, peace in the family, and peace at work and
peace in the world. Moscow had lauched an immense
and lying campaign of propaganda in favour of peace,
and by replying to it in this way through Fatima, Pius
XII was thus once again underlining his confidence both
in Fatima and in the universal character of its message.

In the same month, and doubtless comforted and
reassured by this decision of the Holy Father, Father da
Fonseca, S.J., published a detailed reply to the anti-
Fatima pamphlets of Father Dhanis and the numerous
articles of all those who had blindly repeated his
arguments. His response was firm and well informed,
but it is noteworthy that it did not appear at Rome in the
Civilta Cattolica, the celebrated Jesuit review, but only
in Portugal, in the review *Broteria,* and as a result it
only had an extremely limited diffusion in intellectual
circles in Europe.

On the occasion of his episcopal Jubilee, the Catholics
of the world had offered to the Sovereign Pontiff the
necessary sum for the construction of a new church,
which was dedicated to his patron, St. Eugene. On 2
June 1951, Pius XII proceeded to consecrate the high

altar of this new Roman Basilica, and on 3 June he beatified Pope Pius X. The next day he received in audience a group of Portuguese pilgrims who had given the new basilica the altar for the Virgin, which was dedicated to Our Lady of Fatima. On this occasion, Pius XII spoke at length to them about Fatima:

"From the opening of the Holy Year, we have often had occasion to welcome the ambassadors from the land of Holy Mary, who came to find us and recalled to us the heavenly message of Our Lady of Fatima. It was announced there, but it was intended to be transmitted to the world, and it was almost the anticipated message of a Holy Year without end...

"You intended – and what a happy inspiration of your filial devotion it has been – that the monument in commemoration of our episcopal consecration should at the same time recall the providential coincidence which distinguished it. Perhaps in the secret designs of Providence, this great date, so tremendous in our life, was preparing us for another even greater date, without our being aware of it, when the Lord would place on our shoulders the care of the universal Church. For upon that date, and at the same hour, there was announced in the mountain of Fatima the first apparition of the white Queen of the most Holy Rosary, as if the most Holy Mother wanted to make us understand that, in the stormy years which would envelope our pontificate, and in the midst of one of the greatest crises in the history of the world, we would always have, to surround, protect and guide us, the maternal and vigilant assistance of her who is always victorious in all the battles of God...

"Do not forget, however, that it is the world itself which is the very sick patient today. Ceaselessly implore in its favour the miraculous intervention of the most high Queen of the world, so that the hopes for an era of true peace may be brought to pass as soon as possible, and that the triumph of the Immaculate Heart of Mary will lead more quickly to the triumph of the Heart of

Jesus in the kingdom of God."

At the end of this moving audience, as it is well known, a pilgrim enthusiastically exclaimed: "Long live the Pope of Fatima!" With a smile, Pius XII replied: "That is me!" (Canon Barthas, *Fatima 1917-1968*, p.268).

On 15 September of the same year, Pius XII published the encyclical *Ingruentium Malorum*, entirely consecrated to the devotion of the holy Rosary, which was indicated as "the most efficacious means... to heal the evils which afflict our century ..."

The international congress on the Message of Fatima and peace took place at Lisbon from Sunday 7th to Thursday 11th October, and the opening session was held at the palace of the National Assembly under the presidence of Craveiro Lopes, the president of the Republic. The congress was attended by nearly two thousand delegates from forty-three nations, including five cardinals, more than forty bishops, ministers, ambassadors, members of parliament and theologians.

"On Wednesday," reported Canon Barthas, "they heard the address of Douglas Hyde, the former editor of the *Daily Worker*, the English communist newspaper."

"One day," he told them, "I was sent a copy of a book entitled *Our Lady of Fatima* by Mgr. Ryan. A note which accompanied it drew my attention to pages 90 to 92, which dealt with the question of Russia and Communism, and asked me to refute the arguments. I took the book home and put it in my library between works by Marx, Lenin, Stalin and other Marxist writers. Now, more than three years later, I am a Catholic and this book, with the note clipped to it from the person who sent it to me, is one of my most precious treasures. I have brought it with me to Lisbon and would be delighted to show it to you...

"For me, the message of Our Lady of Fatima is the unique foundation for a hope that soon Communism which divides the world will be vanquished, and that

Russia will be converted. Without this hope, there is no hope whatever, since Communism, in less than thirty years, has dominated a third of humanity and continues on its march... Only this certainty, that prayer and penance are the way of salvation, saves from despair those who know the nature, the strength and the diabolical character of Communism, because Communism is diabolical and is perhaps the worst thing that the world has ever known." (Canon Barthas, *Fatima et les destins du monde*, pp.117-118).

In the evening session, which was presided over by the papal legate, Cardinal Tedeschini, the principal speaker was Mgr. Fulton Sheen, who at that time was auxiliary bishop of New York:

"He demonstrated a striking kind of parallel between the stages in the growth of Russian Communism and the evolution of the mystery of Fatima, from which it indeed seems to be evident that Fatima is the remedy brought from Heaven by the Virgin Mary to heal the world from the infernal toxin of atheistic Marxism" (Canon Barthas, op.cit., p.369).

On the Wednesday, the delegates set out for the sanctuary of the Cova da Iria, on the pilgrimage for the closure of the Holy Year. Nearly one million pilgrims assembled at Fatima, and a large crowd spent the whole night in prayer, enduring a thin and cold rain. More prayers than normal were said for Russia. Salazar's government had invited and paid for the whole Pontifical Russian College of Rome to come on the pilgrimage. At 7 o'clock on the morning of the 13th, a solemn Mass was said for the conversion of Russia, celebrated in the Russo-Byzantine rite by Mgr. Meletieff, the Russian bishop converted from Orthodoxy, with Fr. Wetter, the rector of the Russicum, and Father Koren.

Later, the Cardinal Legate presided over the solemn Mass, in the course of which he gave a homily which made the greatest impression on the hundreds of thousands of pilgrims:

"'Signum Dei! We have seen the sign of God!' Such
was the reflection made by the stupefied crowd on this
13th October 1917. Mary, 'dressed with the sun', had,
so to say, simply shaken the hem of her heavenly
garment for a few seconds. The sun had obeyed her
orders and, in obeying her, had stamped on the message
of Fatima a seal more brilliant than any emperor could
have done. Everything about it is grandiose, all is most
worthy of the Queen of Heaven! It is a marvel which has
never before been seen!

"Nevertheless, and speaking on a purely personal
level, I would like to tell my Portuguese friends, past
and present, and all the pilgrims who are united with
them, of something even more marvellous. I would like
to tell them that another person has seen this miracle,
away from Fatima, quite a few years later, at Rome.
And this person is the pope, Pope Pius XII himself!

"**Was this grace a reward for him? Was this a
sign demonstrating that the definition of the dogma
of the Assumption had been supremely agreeable to
God? Was it a testimony from heaven to
authenticate the connection between the mystery of
Fatima and the centre, the head of the Truth and
of the Catholic Magisterium? It was all three things
at once**... Was not that sign Fatima transported to the
Vatican? Was not that sign the Vatican transformed into
a new Fatima? The binominal Fatima-Vatican was thus
more than ever made manifest during the Holy Year
Jubilee of 1950" (*l'Osservatore Romano*, 18 November
1951).

At the end of the Mass, the Pope again spoke to the
pilgrims by radio, as he had before on 31 October 1942
and on 13 May 1946, and in the course of his address he
stated:

"...It is no longer, or rather, it is no longer only the
Angel of the Lord, it is the Queen of Angels who,
issuing forth with her miraculous statues from the most
celebrated sanctuaries in Christendom, and specially

from this sanctuary of Fatima – where Heaven allowed us to crown her Queen of the world – is making a jubilee visit to all her domains.

"At her passage, in America just as in Europe, in Africa and in India, in Indonesia and in Australia, blessings rain down from Heaven, and marvels of grace are multiplied, in such a way that we can hardly believe what our eyes are seeing. And it is not only the obedient and faithful sons of the Church who redouble their fervour; it is the prodigal sons who return to their paternal home, subdued by the memory of her maternal caresses; we have even seen men still enveloped in the darkness of error, in those countries where the light of the Gospel is only just beginning to shine, waiting for her visit in crowds, rivalling the faithful of Christ, receiving and greeting her with enthusiasm, venerating her, invoking her and obtaining signal graces from her...

"That is why we joyfully agreed to preside in spirit over these solemnities, and we intend to confide this Holy Year to Mary, in a tangible way, so to speak, certain that our thanksgivings, passing through her Immaculate Heart, will be more acceptable to the Lord, and that in her blessed hands the salutary fruits of the Jubilee, far from disappearing promptly, will be conserved, blessed and multiplied.

"In her Message which, as a 'pilgrim', She repeats as She travels throughout the world, Our Lady shows us the certain path of peace, and all the means necessary to obtain it from Heaven, for human means can hardly be trusted. When, with particular insistence, She asks us for the recitation of the Rosary in the family, She seems to tell us that it is in imitation of the Holy Family that one will find the secret of peace in the home. When She exhorts us to look after our neighbour like ourselves, and to pray and sacrifice ourselves for our neighbour's spiritual and temporal welfare, She shows us the truly efficacious way of re-establishing harmony between the social classes.   Finally, when her maternal voice, saddened and suppliant, asks us to make a general and sincere return to a more Christian life, is She not telling us again that it is only through peace with God, and respect for justice and the eternal law, that the edifice of world peace can be solidly established?   For if God does not build it, those who work at it work in vain..."

Our Lady of Syracuse
(see pp. 191–193)

Chapter XII

FATIMA SILENCED, OUR LADY WEEPS

The grandiose ceremonies at the Cova da Iria on 13 October 1951 incontestably raised the diffusion of the message of Fatima to a new height, but nevertheless it cannot be denied that, looking at Fatima in the light of the world situation, an unjustified and illusory optimism was gradually overcoming the majority of the Fatima experts. Professing an absolute confidence in the Holy Father, without any restriction or limit, exactly as if he possessed a double charisma of impeccability in all his acts and infallibility in all domains and on all occasions, they did not even dare to suggest that the Pope had not yet obeyed all the requests of Our Lady. But had he not consecrated the world to the Immaculate Heart of Mary? Yes, but that is all he had done! And so, in order not to run the risk of displeasing him, it was necessary to keep quiet about the other demands of Heaven.

Thus the sweetened version of the great Secret of Our Lady, as first published in 1942, continued to be published for many years, with its lamentable falsifications. For example, in 1947 Father Rolim completely suppressed, in the text of the Secret, the following words of Our Lady: "In order to prevent that, I will come to ask the consecration of Russia to my Immaculate Heart and the communion of reparation of the first five Saturdays of the month". Even Cardinal Cerejeira, in his splendid homily of 30th May 1948 at Madrid, affirmed that "the Queen of peace came to Fatima to ask for *the consecration of the world* to her Immaculate Heart" and this error has been repeated in numerous books, even as late as 1980.

While on the one hand there were those who led people to believe that the Pope had already fulfilled the requests of the Virgin of Fatima, on the other hand there were others who sought to show that her promise for the conversion of Russia was already coming to pass, such as Canon Barthas, John Haffert, in his book *Russia will be converted*, which was published in America in 1951, and Mgr. Fulton Sheen.

This erroneous view of events arose from the forgetfulness that neither the just obedience nor the loving and filial confidence which are due to the Holy Father as Vicar of Christ and as visible head of the Church, can permit the faithful to fail to give primary and absolute respect to the Truth which comes from God. If the Virgin Mary has spoken, and if she has formulated requests, nobody has the right to alter her words, and it is false to attribute to her things which she has not said.

Thus announcing that her promises are about to be fulfilled, when the conditions for their fulfilment have not yet been met by the pastors of the Church, is to deceive the faithful and dishonour Our Lady.

Alas, the cause of Fatima has suffered enormous damage from the errors, the attenuations, the misrepresentations, and the silence of so many of those who could have and should have spoken by simply making themselves the humble echo of the true requests of the Queen of Heaven, for the salvation of the Church and of the world. On this occasion of the memorable pilgrimage to Fatima of 13 October 1951, however, by good fortune Sister Lucia was presented with a favourable opportunity to make her views known. The day after the pilgrimage, in the course of which so many prayers had been offered up for Russia, Father Wetter, S.J., the rector of the Russicum, accompanied by one of the Russian seminarians and Mgr. Meletieff, the converted Russian bishop, visited her at the Carmel of Coimbra. During the interview, Sister Lucia asked: "Would it be possible for you to transmit to the Holy Father (a message) that what Our Lady of Fatima requested has not yet been done?" Father Wetter replied in the affirmative.

The reliable witness, who has given us this information, and who was living at that time in the Russicum, assures us that Father Wetter effectively transmitted this request to the Pope, probably through the intermediary of Father Leiber, who was also a Jesuit, and the private secretary of Pius XII.

In a letter to a friend dated 15 December 1951, Sister Lucia wrote, in confirmation of the above:

"The request of Our Lady concerning Russia has not been carried out. According to what X has informed me, the bishops of Russia have addressed a supplication to the Holy Father requesting the consecration of Russia to the Immaculate Heart of Mary, such as it was asked for by Our Lady..."

However, we now know, from a letter received by the author from Miss Posnoff dated 23 February 1984, that this petition did not request the consecration of Russia "such as it was asked for by Our Lady". In her letter, Miss Posnoff states that **"unfortunately we did not then know that this consecration should be made in union with all the bishops,** for in the text which was in our possession, after the words 'consecration of Russia' there were points of suspension indicating that a few words had been omitted." Despite this regrettable omission, this supplication is moving and vigorously expresses the antagonism between Satan, the prince of this world, and the Immaculate Queen of Heaven, as the following extracts from the text show:

"We, the signatories of this letter, bishops, priests, and lay Catholics of Russia, and likewise the entire College of the Russian Seminary of Rome, the 'Russicum', we all met together in November 1950, for the pilgrimage of the Catholics of Russia on the occasion of the Holy Year...

"In one united body, we dare to ask Your Holiness to specially consecrate our country, Russia, which has suffered so much, to Our Lady, to the Queen of the world, that is to say, to her maternal and Immaculate Heart, pierced by the sword...

"The deliverance of our country, and thereafter of the whole world, from the terrible slavery of bolchevism, cannot be obtained simply by the material forces of arms and money. It is becoming more and more clear that the warfare against God and the Holy Church being undertaken by the bolchevics, is not led only by human forces. These forces have as their source Satan himself and the spirits of darkness under him who carry out their warfare more and more openly; and the hour is not far off when, perhaps, the visage of Satan will appear before us unveiled, and no longer concealed by the human hands which act under his impetus and direction. Mere material arms – money and weapons – are by themselves powerless against the direct action of Satan. Another force is required, another help; it must be a heavenly and supernatural force. This force and this help, we possess it in the Most Holy Virgin...

"In our day we see that the strengthening of materialistic atheism... is equalled by a profound submission to the Most Holy Virgin, with a better understanding of the meaning of this submission. Do not these two parallel movements show where evil is and where can be found the force capable of overcoming it? Evil is Satan, having taken the appearance of Marxist bolchevic atheism, and the force capable of overcoming it is our Holy Queen and protectress, the Mother of our God...

"It is important and necessary that Russia, true Christian Russia, should enter the army of the Most Holy Virgin for the final and definitive struggle against the serpent. That is the pledge of the salvation of humanity. From time immemorial Russia has been called the House of the Most Holy Virgin, and the principal church, which is situated within the walls of the Kremlin – and which was profaned by the bolchevics – is consecrated to her glorious Assumption.

"But who is there at present who could carry out this consecration in the name of Russia profaned and enslaved? We can see only one solution and we express it in our humble request. We ask that this consecration should be carried out by the Vicar of Christ on earth, the successor of the Prince of the Apostles, Peter, the Sovereign Pontiff of the universal Church, the Pope of ancient Rome..."

From the foregoing, it is clear that the representatives of Holy Russia had at least done everything possible to bring about the fulfilment of the requests of the Virgin of Fatima. If we may believe a voluminous Italian work, which was published in 1960, on the consecration of Italy to the Immaculate Heart of Mary, the Most Holy Virgin appeared again to Sister Lucia in May 1952, and deigned to signify that she approved of their supplication: "The Madonna appeared to Lucia: 'Make known to the Holy Father that I am still waiting for the consecration of Russia to my Immaculate Heart. Without this consecration, Russia cannot be converted, and the world cannot have peace'".

The book containing this statement, *Il Pellegrinaggio delle Meraviglie* (p.440), which was published under the auspices of the Italian hierarchy, also states that this message was communicated to Pius XII in June.

Although he had promised Miss Posnoff that he would not oppose the petition of the Russicum, Father Dhanis took up his pen again, doubtless at the instigation of people higher placed than himself in the hierarchy, and near enough to the Holy Father in order to guarantee him impunity. In the June issue of the *Nouvelle Revue Théologique*, he published an article which claimed to refute the corrections which had been published by Father da Fonseca in May of the previous year. It would be necessary to read the whole of this article, which was published in the review of the university of Louvain, to see how subtly it was aimed at dissuading the Pope from carrying out the consecration

of Russia, precisely at the moment when he was being
asked for it with insistence, by stirring up a campaign in
the opposite direction among European intellectual
circles. Father Dhanis quotes again from the article
which he originally published in 1945:

"It is not necessary for lengthy reflection to see that
the Sovereign Pontiff was in a position which made it
practically impossible for him to carry out such a
consecration. As its Head, the Pope can consecrate the
Church to the Immaculate Heart of Mary: as Vicar of
Our Lord Jesus Christ, and charged by virtue of this
office with leading the whole human race to salvation,
he can consecrate the world to the Immaculate Heart:
speaking in absolute terms, he can also consecrate to it a
country such as Russia, since Russia is part of the
world.

"But in actual fact these matters are more difficult than
that. Schismatic, from the point of view of religious
unity, and Marxist from the point of view of political
unity, Russia could not be consecrated by the Pope
without such an act taking on an appearance of defiance,
both with regard to the separated hierarchy, and with
regard to the Union of Soviet Republics. This rendered
the consecration practically unrealizeable. It is clear
here that it is simply a question of the moral
impossibility of the consecration, by reason of the
reactions which it would normally arouse... **But could
the Most Holy Virgin have asked for a consecration
which, if interpreted according to the strict
meaning of the words, was practically
unrealizeable?... This question would appear to call
for a negative response.**"

In a word, Father Dhanis reaffirms his thesis: the
consecration of Russia cannot be done, and that is so
obvious that one is led to doubt whether the Blessed
Virgin did in fact make such a request.

Happily, however, by the time this article appeared,
Pius XII had already instructed Father Hermann, a

Jesuit of the Oriental Institute, to prepare the text by which he would consecrate Russia to the Immaculate Heart of Mary. On 30 June, he received the Russicum in audience, doubtless to announce that he had acceded to its request, and on 7 July 1952, on the occasion of the feast of Saints Cyril and Methodius, the glorious apostles of the Slav peoples, he published the apostolic letter *Sacro vergente anno*, from which the following essential passages have been taken:

"Dear people of Russia, health and peace in the Lord!

"While the Holy Year was happily drawing to a conclusion, after it had been given to us by a divine disposition to solemnly define the dogma of the Assumption into Heaven, body and soul, of the Holy Mother of God, the Virgin Mary, we received numerous expressions of the most lively exultation from people all over the world; many of them sent us letters in thanksgiving, in which they also earnestly begged us to consecrate the whole Russian people, which is experiencing such suffering at this moment, to the Immaculate Heart of the Virgin Mary.

"These supplications were particularly pleasing to us, for if our paternal affection embraces all people, it is addressed in a particular manner to those who, although separated for the most part from the Apostolic See by the vicissitudes of history, nevertheless still retain the name of Christian, but find themselves in such a situation that it is very difficult for them to hear our voice and to know the teachings of Catholic doctrine, and that they are even pushed by deceitful and pernicious contrivances to reject faith in and even the very idea of God".

In the course of a long historical resumé, the Pope recalled the relations between Russia and the Sovereign Pontiffs, and finally mentioned the ceremony of 19 March 1930, at Saint Peter's, Rome, when Pope Pius XI had decided that henceforth the prayers after Mass should be offered for the conversion of Russia. Pius XII then went on: "...When it is a question of defending the cause of religion, the truth, and justice and Christian civilization, we certainly cannot keep quiet... Doubtless we have condemned and rejected — as the duty of our office demands — the errors which the instigators of atheistic Communism teach, or which they do their utmost to propagate, for the greatest wrong and the detriment of the citizens; but, far from rejecting the wayward, we desire their return to the straight path of the truth. Even more: we have unmasked these falsehoods, which are often adorned with a semblance of the truth, because we love you with the heart of a father and we seek your well-being...

"We know that many of you preserve the Christian faith in the secret sanctuary of your own conscience... We know furthermore, and that is for us a great hope and a great consolation, that you love and honour with ardent affection the Virgin Mary, Mother of God, and that you venerate her images. We know that in the city of Moscow itself there is a temple — alas, withdrawn from divine worship — which is dedicated to the Assumption of the Blessed Virgin Mary into heaven; and this is a very clear testimony to the love which your ancestors and you yourselves bear to the Most Holy Mother of God...

"So that our fervent prayers and yours should more easily be answered, and to give you a special sign of our particular benevolence, **just as some years ago we consecrated the whole human race to the Immaculate Heart of the Virgin Mary, Mother of God, so today we consecrate and we dedicate in a very special manner all the peoples of Russia to this Immaculate Heart**... and we implore this most clement Mother to obtain from her divine Son heavenly light for your minds, and for your souls the supernatural strength and courage by which you will be able to avert and surmount all errors and godlessness."

It is clear that by pronouncing this consecration, in which Russia was at last explicitly mentioned by name,

Pius XII was secretly striving to fulfil the requests of the Virgin of Fatima. By this pronouncement, he struck with a formal contradiction the chidings of Father Dhanis, who claimed that the request transmitted by Sister Lucia was "practically unrealizeable".

From henceforward nobody could any longer say that this consecration of Russia, and of Russia alone, designated as such by name, was impossible. From this point of view, *Sacro vergente anno* marks a new and very important stage in the accomplishment of the message of Fatima by the Sovereign Pontiffs. But, unfortunately, it was still only a half-measure.

Let us hear the authoritative opinion of Father Alonso on this precise point, as to whether, in *Sacro vergente anno*, the Holy Father carried out all the conditions requested by Heaven and communicated to Sister Lucia. "Historically, no", says Father Alonso, on page 56 of his book *Marie sous le symbole du Coeur*, published in 1973.

What then was lacking in this new act of the Sovereign Pontiff, so that it did not correspond perfectly with the designs of God as revealed at Fatima? The answer is very clear:

1. Pius XII made no reference to the request of Our Lady – which was nevertheless so pressing, and which is also intended to contribute powerfully to obtaining from God the miracle of the conversion of Russia – for the practice, which is so simple and so salutary for souls, of the devotion of reparation of the five first Saturdays of the month.

2. The solemn act of reparation, which is requested jointly with the consecration of Russia, is only indirectly suggested in the Apostolic Letter.

3. Finally and above all, the Pope did not give all the Catholic bishops of the world the order to unite with him in this solemn act of reparation and consecration.

In consequence, the consecration of Russia on 7 July 1952 – which was not distinguished by any special ceremony — was lacking in that solemnity required for it to correspond in the most explicit manner possible with its supernatural end. When He set out his great design of mercy for our century, Our Lord told His messenger, in May 1936: "I want My whole Church to acknowledge that consecration (of Russia) as a triumph of the Immaculate Heart of Mary, so that it may extend its cult later on and put the devotion to this Immaculate Heart beside the devotion to My Sacred Heart."

No, alas, the truth is that after this act of 7 July 1952, the Church was still a long way from having fully corresponded with the divine plan of grace and mercy for our times. Can one say that Pius XII was not fully informed, and that he did not know that he should have carried out the consecration in union with the bishops of the entire world? It is not yet possible to answer that question, but it does seem very unlikely that he was completely unaware of the precise details of the requests of Our Lady. He had received so many previous and more explicit approaches! Mgr. da Silva had written to Pius XI in 1937; Sister Lucia had written in 1940 and 1942; she had made public declarations in 1943, and in 1946 to Father Jongen and to W.T. Walsh, among others, and doubtless several requests had been sent directly to the Pope after that.

It is true that nobody had made a public, official, clear and precise request to Pius XII to carry out the consecration in union with all the bishops of the world, in the way that Our Lady had required, and that is very regrettable. But Pius XII must surely have heard it spoken about on several occasions. If he had decided to correspond completely to the wishes of the Virgin of Fatima, he would only have had to ask Father da Fonseca — who had prepared his radio broadcasts to the pilgrims of Fatima on 31 October 1942 and on 13 May 1946 - order to learn from him everything that was required. Furthermore, Pius XII was well aware that the seer of Fatima had but lately wanted to meet him in order to speak with him personally.

In a word, one is left instead with the impression that the offensive of Father Dhanis, under the cover of his powerful protectors, had come to fruition. This impression is confirmed by Father Schweigl, the Austrian Jesuit (1894-1964) who was professor at the Gregorian University and at the Russicum, and who was very well informed on everything to do with the consecration of Russia. In his book *Fatima e la conversione della Russia*, which was published by the Pontifical Russian College in 1956, he states that the great Secret "seems to suppose a victorious, triumphant, but difficult and heroic decision" by the Holy Father. "In actual fact, the Holy Father consecrated the peoples of Russia in a special way to the Immaculate Heart of Mary on 7 July 1952, although many circles were against the advisability of such a consecration" (p. 15).

It is a remarkable fact that in his Letter *Sacro vergente anno*, there is not the least mention nor even the slightest veiled allusion to the message of Fatima. This silence must certainly have been deliberate. Presumably Pius XII did not want to be accused of having carried out this act of consecration of Russia in response to a "private revelation".

In a text which was distributed in 1963 to the Council Fathers, entitled *Immaculatum Cor Mariae et Russia*, Father Schweigl relates how he received permission from Pius XII on 27 March 1952 to talk with Sister Lucia of Fatima "about thirty-one questions referring to the conversion of Russia". However, it is important to underline the fact that he did not leave for Portugal until 17 August, or more than one month after the publication of *Sacro vergente anno*. Elsewhere, Father Alonso records: "On 2 September 1952, authorised by the Holy Office, as he himself declared, Father Schweigl questioned Lucia" (*Historia da Literatura Sobre Fatima*, p. 60). What happened at this interrogation? We do not know, for, in Father Schweigl's own words, as published in the text which was distributed to the Council Fathers in 1963, "in 1952, the Archbishop of Coimbra demanded that the replies given by Sister Lucia should not be published without an authorisation from the Holy Office. Up to this moment, this authorisation has not yet been given."

Why did the Holy Office not permit this interrogation to be divulged? It is not difficult to guess the answer: Questioned by Father Schweigl, Sister Lucia must surely have explained to him in what manner the act of 7 July 1952 was still incomplete, and what remained to be done in order to truly comply with the designs of Heaven. It is also practically certain that Father Schweigl, a holy priest who had a great devotion for Our Lady of Fatima, faithfully transmitted to the Holy Father the information which he had received. But it was too late. One has the annoying impression that in the mind of Pius XII, *Sacro vergente anno* was some sort of stopping-point. If this is so, then it is possible that the mission of Father Schweigl, in the autumn of 1952, rather than being a request for information, consisted perhaps in giving precise orders at Coimbra, at Leiria and at Lisbon, that there should be no further public demand for this consecration of Russia, which they wished to consider at Rome as having already been done.

However that may be, this summer of 1952 certainly marks a new turning-point in the pontificate of Pius XII. It was also just at this precise moment that he began to suffer severely from an illness. According to his own doctor, Galeazzi-Lisi: "His health kept quite good up until the end of the month of August 1952, when all of a sudden he began to show the symptoms of a grave intoxication". The doctor stated that his stomach developed serious troubles, which accentuated in the course of time.

On 15 December 1952, in his encyclical *Orientales Ecclesias*, devoted to the persecutions undergone by the countries of the East, the Pope made a brief allusion to the consecration of Russia to the Immaculate Heart of Mary, which he had carried out on 7 July. Thereafter he did not mention it again.

More than a year went by, and then once again the Virgin intervened. From 29 August to 1 September 1953, she came, silently this time, at Syracuse, to make known her immense sadness. The facts are simple and clear, and the miracle is absolutely incontestable, and scientifically proven. In fact never before, perhaps, has a divine intervention been so rapidly recognised and declared authentic by the ecclesiastical authorities.

But this time the Virgin did not come to give the world a new message, new secrets or new prophecies. Nor did she make new requests. No; she came solely to recall, in the most convincing and remarkable manner possible, the essence of the message of Fatima, namely: the revelation of 13 June 1917, in which she showed the children her Immaculate Heart, grieved by the sins of men and asking for reparation.

The prodigy took place at Syracuse in Sicily, on the octave day of the feast of the Immaculate Heart of Mary, in the room of a very humble house in the poor quarter of the town. The young couple to whom it belonged had been given a little statue of the Virgin Mary at their marriage some months before, and they had put it up on the wall. It was a representation of the Virgin, showing her Heart surrounded by thorns and with flames rising up out of it as if it was on fire, like in the apparitions of Our Lady of Fatima on 13 June 1917, and then at Pontevedra and at Tuy in 1925 and 1929.

On that Saturday 29 August, this humble but moving image suddenly started to weep real tears. The tears poured down her cheeks on six or seven occasions in the morning, and she wept again in the evening not long after the husband had returned from his work in the field. On the next two days the same prodigy was seen by thousands of people, not only in the couple's house but also outside, on the wall of the courtyard, and then on a little altar situated opposite. On Tuesday 1 September, the last day on which the statue wept, the phenomenon was closely examined by a commission of experts which had been appointed by the archbishop. As soon as the expert examination was concluded, the prodigy ceased. One week later Syracuse celebrated the birthday of Our Lady, who was patron of the cathedral and of the town, while in Rome the Pope published his encyclical *Fulgens Corona*, in which he announced the Marian Year to commemorate the centenary of the definition of the dogma of the Immaculate Conception.

On 9 September, the laboratory published a detailed report of the analysis which had been carried out on the liquid which came out of the eyes of the little plaster statue. The conclusion was amazing: the liquid was no different from human tears. In the months of September and October, more than a million people came on pilgrimage to the miraculous image and on 12 December, scarcely three months after the event, the Sicilian hierarchy, gathered round Cardinal Ruffini, pronounced the miracle to be authentic in an offical communiqué. Several weeks after the event, the Archbishop of Syracuse declared: "If the Madonna wept tears, she did it to reproach us, or at least to give us a grave warning" (Canon O. Musumeci, *À Syracuse, la Madone a pleuré*, p.146). "Everyone wants to know" said Cardinal Ruffini, **"why the most Holy Virgin wept in this way for four long days... if we recall the celebrated apparitions of Lourdes and of Fatima, the reply is easy... she wept in Sicily, at Syracuse, because here her tears would not flow in vain; because here a multitude of souls would strive to console her and to bring others to console her"** (Ibid, pp.195-196).

Yes, incontestably it is the message of the Immaculate Virgin to Sister Lucia, at Fatima, at Tuy and at Pontevedra, which best expresses the significance of these tears. A simple statue of plaster wept

miraculous tears because the Virgin knew that sin and
apostasy were increasing throughout the world, souls
were being lost, the errors of Russia were continuing to
spread everywhere, raising up wars and persecutions,
and still her simple requests were not being fulfilled by
the Church herself.

Meanwhile, in February 1953, seven months after
the consecration of Russia to the Immaculate Heart of
Mary by Pius XII, Father Dhanis once again took up his
pen against Fatima.   In that same month, Father
Veloso, a Portuguese Jesuit friend of Father da Fonseca,
published in the Portuguese Jesuit review, *Broteria*, a
severe and damaging criticism of Father Dhanis' previous
article. The adversary of Fatima wanted to have the last
word, and he wrote a reply, but it was published, not in
the *Nouvelle Revue Théologique* of Louvain, as in the
previous year, nor in *Broteria*, the Portuguese Jesuit
review in which he had just been attacked, but at Rome,
in the semi-official *Civilta Cattolica*. When one realises
that the director of the great Jesuit review used to meet
the Pope every fortnight, one may well imagine that it
was most probably Pius XII himself, in agreement with
Father Janssens, the General of the Society of Jesus,
who granted Dhanis the honour and the privilege of
issuing his reply in the columns of the *Civilta Cattolica*,
on condition that he put an end to the controversy which
had caused a scandalous confrontation between several
members of the Society.

The article appeared in May 1953, and despite
appearances, by making this concession – which is what
in fact he had done – Pius XII had once again yielded to
the anti-Fatima camp. At one stroke, the serious and
ardent Jesuit champion of Fatima, Father da Fonseca,
was denied access to one of the most prestigious,
influential, and widely-circulating reviews of the Holy
See, while the supposed advocate of Our Lady was left
complete freedom to continue his deeply subtle attacks
and his utterly unjustified criticisms of the great Secret.

No doubt Pius XII was hoping that this would prove a satisfactory compromise, but that did not turn out to be the case, for the publication of this article was quite disastrous for the cause of Fatima. Dhanis was an extremely skilful propagandist, and while his real and ultimate objective was to raise doubts everywhere concerning the subject which he described as Fatima Part II, he succeeded in introducing these doubts in a manner which made them appear as if they were the sound middle way: completely prudent, moderate, objective and reasonable. He made out that nobody had a greater devotion to Our Lady than himself, and that he was only concerned with the truth and with rendering the greatest possible service to the Virgin of Fatima. Furthermore, he managed to make it appear that, as regards the essentials, he was in complete agreement with his former adversaries, for whom he did not seem to harbour any animosity. Neither Father Veloso nor Father da Fonseca were able to reply and correct this article, and so Father Dhanis was left in possession of the field, having had the last word.

Indeed, it would appear from the fact that the Pope had already kept silence on Fatima for more than a year, that Dhanis had won over Pius XII to his point of view. The broadcast addressed to the pilgrims of Fatima on 13 October 1951 was the last solemn act of the Pope in favour of Fatima. Thereafter, it is only necessary to examine the pontifical documents for the last seven years of his reign, to realise the undeniable fact that in these years relations between Rome and Fatima became notably cooler.

There was not a single allusion to Fatima in 1952 – not even, as we have seen, in his encyclical *Sacro Vergente anno*, in which he consecrated Russia to the Immaculate Heart of Mary. In April 1953, there was only the very briefest mention of Our Lady of Fatima in the Pope's broadcast to the farmers of Colombia, even though it was under this title that Our Lady was invoked

as their patron. And on 8 September, in the encyclical
Fulgens corona announcing the forthcoming Marian
Year, he evoked the apparitions of Lourdes at some
length, but said not a word about Fatima. In 1954, the
Marian Year, the public mentions of Fatima in the
pontifical addresses are almost equally rare, and certainly
equally as brief. In the encyclical *Ad Coeli Reginam*, he
simply recalled his broadcast in 1946 "for the coronation
of the miraculous statue of Fatima", and in his broadcast
to the Marian Congress in Colombia, on 8 December, he
alluded without comment to "the inauguration of the
national monument to Our Lady of Fatima". And that
was all. 1955 saw the categorical and formal refusal of
Rome to grant the request of the whole Portuguese
hierarchy, submitted on 13 July 1955, for a feast in
honour of "The Apparition of the Blessed Virgin of the
Most Holy Rosary", to be celebrated on 13 May with its
proper office, a draft of which was submitted at the same
time for the approval of the Congregation of Rites.

The obstacle was to be found at Rome, among the
anti-Fatima party, for whom Dhanis had simply served
as spokesman. In this group, there was Mgr. Montini,
who was still very influential, although he had been
removed from his ofice as pro-Secretary of State the
previous November; Mgr. Dell'Acqua, the new
substitute; Father Bea, the Pope's confessor, and already
secretly strongly in favour of ecumenism and ready for
any concessions, especially in the field of Marian
devotion; Father Janssens, the General of the Jesuits;
and Dhanis himself, who by this time had become the
semi-official expert of the Society – if not for all the
Vatican – on everything which concerned Fatima.

It was also about this time, as John Haffert relates on
page 54 of his book, *Fatima, World Apostolate* (1984),
that Sister Lucia found she was much more closely
surveyed, and reduced to almost total silence: "the Pope
decided that only those persons who had already seen her
could see her again without the express authorisation of

the Holy See".

1956 saw the publication of the encyclical *Haurietas aquas*, a magnificent treasure of doctrine on the cult of the Sacred Heart of Jesus. However, even though the Pope ended his encyclical by urging the faithful to associate the cult of the Sacred Heart of Jesus with devotion to the Immaculate Heart of Mary, and although, in speaking of Mary, he expounded the principal themes revealed by Our Lady at Fatima, nevertheless Fatima was not mentioned, and there was not the slightest attempt to recall – as Cardinal Cerejeira loved to do so frequently – that Fatima, in our century, is to the Immaculate Heart of Mary what Paray-le-Monial was to the cult of the Sacred Heart of Jesus.

It is important to mention the question of the Third Secret at this point, because we know, from Cardinal Ottaviani, that Pius XII could have read it from 1944 onwards, and because a number of other eminent witnesses, such as Cardinal Cerejeira, Canon Galamba and Canon Barthas, testify that Sister Lucia made Bishop da Silva promise that it would be opened and read to the world, either upon her death or in 1960, whichever came to pass first. When Canon Barthas asked her why, she replied: "Because the Blessed Virgin wishes it so".

Father Alonso tells us that the envelope containing the Third Secret arrived in Rome on 16 April 1957 ("De nuevo el Secreto de Fatima", *Ephemerides Mariologicae*, 1982, p.86).

We know that Pius XII considered this third Secret of great importance. On 14 May 1957, barely a month later, the journalist Robert Serrou was allowed into his apartments for research on an article which was later published in Paris-Match. In a letter dated 5 January 1985, he told me that Sister Pascalina, who was in charge of the Pope's household at that time, pointed to the small box on his desk, bearing a label with the words "Secret of the Holy Office", and said; "In that box is the third Secret of Fatima".

Disconcerting though it may seem, there is absolutely no proof or even the least indication which enables us to state that Pius XII did indeed read the last Secret of Fatima. On the contrary, the evidence of Cardinal Ottaviani, in his allocution on the Secret of Fatima on 11 February 1967, and that of Mgr. Loris Capovilla, who was the private secretary and confidant of Pope John XXIII, clearly agrees in stating that the envelope was transmitted to John XXIII "still sealed."

In 1957, there were only the briefest of allusions to Fatima, and throughout 1958 the very name of Fatima was completely absent from papal discourses, although, in its centenary year, Pius XII spoke frequently of the apparitions at Lourdes. However, not once did he take the opportunity, on these occasions, to recall the magnificent continuity between the manifestation of the Immaculate Conception in 1858 and the revelation of the Immaculate Heart of Mary at Fatima in 1917.

Even more astonishing was the silence on the occasion of the first "Congress of the states of perfection" which was held at Lisbon from 8 to 14 April 1958, presided over by Cardinal Cerejeira and attended by numerous bishops and 1500 representatives of a hundred orders and religious congregations. Pius XII addressed a long letter to the members of this Portuguese congress, in which he first of all recalled the bitter anti-Christian persecution which they had suffered in the 18th century, and then in 1834 and 1910; but thereafter he referred to the marvellous Catholic renaissance which had taken place in Portugal without even mentioning the name of Fatima! The omission of the apparitions of Fatima, in such a context, cannot have been a simple mistake. It must have been deliberate.

Likewise, the Vatican kept silence when, on 13 May 1958, 500,000 pilgrims gathered at the Cova da Iria for the blessing of the colossal statue of the Immaculate Heart of Mary which had been carved by Fr. McGlynn, and which was to be placed on the front of the basilica.

What a sad drama it all is! The old bishop of Leiria-Fatima, Mgr. da Silva, died on 4 December 1957, without having read the Secret, for fear of his responsibilities. Less than a year later, on 9 October 1958, Pope Pius XII followed him to the tomb, without having read the Secret. As Sister Lucia told Father Fuentes on 26 December 1957, the Holy Father, like the Bishop of Fatima, could have known the Secret of Fatima "by the wish of the Most Holy Virgin, but they did not want to, in order not to be influenced."

There remained Cardinal Cerejeira. On the death of Mgr. da Silva in December 1957, he should have become the depositary of the Secret and divulged it himself in 1960, as he had publicly announced he intended to do. But he was prevented from fulfilling the wish of Our Lady by the communication from the Holy Office which, as we have seen, ordered the Secret to be transferred to Rome. When the year in which Our Lady wished that it should be made public finally arrived, to the great surprise, indignation and scandal of the faithful a completely anonymous, inconsistent and even contradictory Vatican communiqué was suddenly issued on 8 February 1960, stating that "the text of the letter of Sister Lucia would not be revealed" and that "it is probable that the Secret of Fatima will never be made public". On 24 February 1960, it was reported in the Portuguese Catholic daily, *Novidades,* that Cardinal Cerejeira said of this communiqué: "I know nothing at all about it, and I state categorically that I was not consulted about the subject."

In this fateful year of 1960, the year in which the Virgin had said that she wanted the Secret to be made known, there was one last attempt to break the silence being imposed on Fatima by Rome. The day after the pilgrimage of 13 May, Mgr. Venancio, the new Bishop of Leiria-Fatima, took the courageous decision to send an appeal to all the bishops of the world, without referring to the Pope, whom he simply intended to inform afterwards. In his letter, of 17 May 1960, Mgr. Venancio invited pilgrims to Fatima to make a special effort of prayer and penance on the night of 12-13 October of that year, in reparation for the rising tide of sin and the indifference of so many Christians; and he appealed to the bishops of the world to invite their faithful to unite with the pilgrims of Fatima in similar acts of reparation, in order to "help remove the obstacles which had prevented the previous solemn acts of consecration of the Sovereign Pontiff from achieving their full efficacy, for the conversion of Russia, so dear to the Mother of God, and for obtaining a true peace".

Alas, Pope John XXIII remained insensible to all the requests which had been addressed to him: the last Secret of Our Lady was not to be revealed; he did not even deign to renew the consecration of the world and of Russia to the Immaculate Heart of Mary; nor did he agree to broadcast a message to the pilgrims of Fatima. The Vatican Secretary of State simply sent a telegram, by order of the Sovereign Pontiff, in which he granted them his apostolic blessing.

As can be seen from the evidence which has been set out in the foregoing pages, it is our painful and inescapable conclusion that, **during the last years of the reign of Pius XII, and in the early years of the pontificate of John XXIII, one can no longer find in any Roman document or in any pontifical address, a single phrase, not even a single word which might displease the adversaries of Fatima, and which does not perfectly coincide with the thesis of Father Dhanis:** acceptance of Fatima I and of the pilgrimage, silence on Fatima II and the great Secret.

The formidable success of Dhanis and his party is not simply accountable to his pen and his protectors in high places. In his work *Fatima y la Critica*, Father Alonso cites a very extensive list, covering almost thirty pages (pp. 407-435), of all those persons, drawn from almost

every country in Europe, who have repeated his thesis –
including Otto Karrer, Schäzler, Brennikmeyer, de
Letter, Martindale, Stahlin, Karl Rahner,
Kloppenburg, Baumann, Bernardus, and so on.

Father Alonso is the renowned Spanish Claretian and
Marian theologian who was commissioned in 1966 by the
Bishop of Leiria to write the definitive history of
Fatima. This he achieved in a monumental work of
fourteen volumes, which includes a large number of
hitherto unknown letters, documents and texts, but
unfortunately for the good of souls who urgently need to
know the whole truth of the history of Fatima, it still
remains unpublished. However, before his death on 12
December 1982, Father Alonso was able to publish the
essential parts of his great work of research in a number
of books and articles. In his *Fatima y la Critica*, this is
the conclusion he reaches on the nature and effect of the
writings of the great opponent of Fatima:

**"Dhanis has forged a hypothesis which is as vast
as a cathedral, and which can ruin, not only the
history of the apparitions of the Angel, but also -
for why should not the hypothesis be carried to its
logical conclusion? - absolutely the whole history
of Fatima"** (p.403).

However, concealed in the mystery of Fatima, and
transcending all the considerations that have been
examined hitherto, is the greatest of all its secrets, more
important even than the still-unpublished Third Secret.
This "secret of secrets" contains what may be called the
soul of the revelations of Fatima, and their incandescent
furnace whose ardent flames cast their bright light upon
our gloomy times. It is the secret which little Jacinta
recalled to her cousin, as if making her will, before
leaving her to die:

"It will not be long now before I go to heaven. You
will remain here to make known that God wishes to
establish in the world devotion to the Immaculate Heart
of Mary. When you are to say this, don't go and hide.

Tell everybody that God grants us graces through the Immaculate Heart of Mary; that people are to ask her for them; and that the heart of Jesus wants the Immaculate Heart of Mary to be venerated at His side..." (*Fatima in Lucia's Own Words*, pp. 111, 112).

This is the admirable secret of the mediation of grace and mercy of the Immaculate Heart of our Mother in heaven. As St. Louis de Montfort states in his *Secret of Mary*, this is a secret "which is almost unknown throughout the whole world", and which, nevertheless, is addressed to everyone. As Sister Lucia says so well :

"I always remember the great promise (of Our Lady) which fills me with joy : 'I will never forsake you. My Immaculate Heart will be your refuge and the way that will lead you to God.' I believe that this promise is not for me alone, but for all those souls who wish to take refuge in the Heart of their heavenly Mother and allow themselves to be led along the paths indicated by her..." (Letter of 14 April 1945, quoted on pp. 62-63 of *Fatima e o Coracao de Maria* by Father A. M. Martins, S.J.).

In this way we will work in the most efficacious way possible to hasten the hour of the triumph of the Immaculate Heart of Mary, which is the necessary prelude to the universal reign of the Sacred Heart of Jesus :

"Modern times are dominated by Satan", said St. Maximilian Kolbe, "and they will be more so in the future. The conflict with Hell cannot be engaged in by men, even the most clever. The Immaculata alone has received from God the promise of victory over Satan. But, in the glory of Heaven, she has need of our collaboration today. She seeks for souls who consecrate themselves entirely to Her and who become, in her hands, a force to overcome Satan and instruments to establish the kingdom of God".

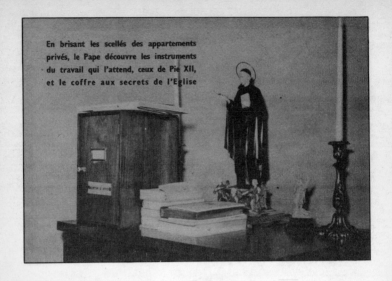

En brisant les scellés des appartements privés, le Pape découvre les instruments du travail qui l'attend, ceux de Pie XII, et le coffre aux secrets de l'Eglise

Pope Pius XII's desk, showing the little chest where the Third Secret of Fatima was kept from 1957. This photo was published on page 82 of *Paris-Match* of 18 October 1958 (see p.196).

Mgr. da Silva, the Bishop of Leiria-Fatima, who kept the Third Secret from 1944 to 1957. On the envelope containing it, which can be seen in the front of the picture, he wrote in his own hand:

Este envelope com o seu conteudo sera entregue a Sua Eminencia O Sr. Cardeal D.Manuel, Patriarca de Lisboa, depois da minha morte.
Leiria, 8 de Dezembro de 1945
José, Bispo de Leiria.

Appendix

THE THIRD SECRET OF FATIMA

We are including a short appendix on Brother Michel's treatment of the Third Secret of Fatima because, as he explains in it, Cardinal Ratzinger, who has read the Third Secret, and the Bishop of Leiria-Fatima have both told us, in August and September 1984, that the Third Secret specifies the crisis of faith which the Church is now undergoing. Brother Michel cites a number of very important facts which have emerged since the reign of Pope Pius XII, and concludes that the Third Secret "is at the heart of the Message of Fatima", and that "it is urgent for the good of the Church that it be revealed according to the wish of the Blessed Virgin".

Some 190 out of a total of 570 pages of his volume III, on the Third Secret of Fatima, are exclusively devoted to elucidating the whole mystery of the final and as yet unpublished Secret of Our Lady; fortunately, Brother Michel himself has made a summary of his extensive study on the Third Secret, which he read as an address to the Fatima Symposium at Rome in November 1985. An English translation of this address was issued by Augustine Publishing Company in September 1986, and it is from this 37-page pamphlet, entitled *The Third Secret of Fatima*, that the resumé which follows has been condensed.

It was in July/August 1941, in her third Memoir, that Sister Lucia mentioned for the first time the division of the Secret of Fatima into three distinct parts. The first is the vision of Hell and the designation of the Immaculate Heart of Mary as the supreme remedy offered by God to humanity for the salvation of souls. "In order to save them, God wishes to establish in the world devotion to My Immaculate Heart". The second part of the Secret is the great prophecy concerning a miraculous peace which God wishes to grant to the world through the consecration of Russia to the Immaculate Heart of Mary, and the practice of the Communion of Reparation on the five first Saturdays of the month. "If people attend to my requests, Russia will be converted and the world will have peace". There is also the announcement of terrible punishments if people persist in not obeying her requests.

After considerable correspondence with her bishop, followed by a terrible spiritual anguish which she suffered for almost three months, and only overcame after a further apparition of the Blessed Virgin, Sister Lucia was eventually able to write out the text of the Third Secret in January 1944. The immediate recipient of the Secret was Bishop da Silva , and Sister Lucia told him from the Blessed Virgin that he could have read it at once. Unfortunately, frightened by the responsibility that he would have to assume, he did not dare to do so, he did not wish to have knowledge of it. He then tried to commit it to the Holy Office, but Rome refused to receive it. It was then agreed that if Bishop da Silva happened to die, the envelope containing the Secret, which had been sealed with wax, would be entrusted to Cardinal Cerejeira, the Patriarch of Lisbon.

It is therefore false to say, as has so often been repeated after 1960, that the Third Secret is destined explicitly and exclusively for the Holy Father !

However, I provide several proofs in my book that Sister Lucia wanted Pope Pius XII to know the Secret without further delay. Unfortunately, that did not happen. But I can state with absolute certitude that Sister Lucia made Bishop da Silva promise, in the words of Canon Galamba, "that the Third Secret would be opened and read to the world upon her death or in 1960, whichever would happen first".

Finally, my book contains all the necessary

proofs to show that it was the Will of God that the final Secret of Our Lady should be filially believed by all the pastors of the Church, and made public to the faithful at the latest by 1960 because, in the words of Sister Lucia, "the Blessed Virgin wishes it so" and because, as Sister Lucia further explained, "it would become clearer at that time".

We know that the Third Secret is not very long, probably about 20 to 25 lines, or about the same length as the Second Secret, because Bishop Venancio told me himself that he held the envelope up to the light, and could see inside a little sheet of which he measured the exact size. This allows us to reject as certainly inauthentic several texts which are much too long, and which some forgers have tried to foist upon the public as being the true Secret of Fatima.

On 16 April 1957, the sealed envelope arrived in Rome, at the request of the Holy Office, and it was placed in the office of Pope Pius XII, in a little chest bearing the note, "Secret of the Holy Office".

It is almost certain that Pope Pius XII did not read the Secret, since both Cardinal Ottaviani and Mgr. Capovilla, the Secretary of Pope John XXIII, stated that the envelope was still sealed when John XIII opened it in 1959, one year after the death of Pius XII. One understands, therefore, the solemn words of Sister Lucia to Father Fuentes, at that time Postulator of the beatification causes of Jacinta and Francisco, on 26 December 1957:

"The Blessed Virgin is very sad, for no one attaches any importance to her Message. Neither the good nor the bad... Only the Holy Father and the Bishop of Fatima would be able to know it in accordance with the will of the Blessed Virgin. But they have not willed to know it as they did not want to be influenced".

Pope John XXIII had the envelope containing the Third Secret brought to him at Castelgandolfo on 17 August 1959, and he read it a few days later. Renowned

Fatima experts throughout the world had for years been expecting the final Secret to be revealed by 1960 at the latest, and the consent of Pope Pius XII in 1942 to the disclosure of the first two secrets constituted a precedent. Suddenly, on 8 February 1960 a completely anonymous, inconsistent and even contradictory Vatican communiqué was issued to a Portuguese press agency, stating that the Third Secret would not be published, and that it would probably never be disclosed. The proper Portuguese authorities were completely disregarded, as neither Bishop Venancio of Fatima-Leiria nor Cardinal Cerejeira had been consulted or notified by Rome. Bishop Venancio attempted to appeal to all the bishops of the world, but the Vatican turned a deaf ear to this proposal, and nothing came of it.

Following Pope John XXIII, both Pope Paul VI and Pope John Paul II have read the Third Secret, but did not choose to make it public. Is it therefore possible to know its essential content? We know four fundamental facts about it, which help us to uncover the mystery.

First, we know its context, since we know three out of four parts of its composite entity. Secondly, we know the dramatic circumstances in which it was written down and which themselves reveal its tragic gravity. Thirdly, we know that it is purely on account of its content that successive popes have refused to disclose it. Lastly, there is a timetable in the realization of the prophecies of Fatima from which we can deduce with certainty that we are now in the period of which it speaks. Sister Lucia tells us that the Virgin asked that the Secret be made public in 1960 because at that time "the Message will appear more clear" – in other words, because it is beginning to be fulfilled. But it has not yet reached its conclusion because Russia has not yet been consecrated to the Immaculate Heart of Mary in the way specified by Our Lady, and as it will be one day. Hence we are now living through the events announced by the Third Secret.

This last conclusion has itself been confirmed by two recent declarations of the utmost importance.

On 10 September 1984, Mgr. Cosme do Amaral, the present Bishop of Leiria-Fatima, declared in the great hall of the Technical University of Vienna, in the course of a session of questions and answers:

"The Secret of Fatima speaks neither of atomic bombs nor of nuclear warheads, nor of SS20 missiles. Its content concerns only our faith. To identify the Secret with catastrophic announcements or with a nuclear holocaust is to distort the meaning of the Message. The loss of faith of a continent is worse than the annihilation of a nation; and it is true that the faith is continually diminishing in Europe".

In other words, the Bishop of Fatima has now publicly confirmed the thesis of the celebrated and official Fatima historian, Father Alonso: it is a terrible crisis within the Church, and the loss of the faith, which the Immaculate Virgin announced, precisely for our era, if her requests were not sufficiently carried out.

Sister Lucia herself has written tellingly of how "so many people let themselves be dominated by the diabolical wave that is sweeping the world, and are blinded to the point of being incapable of seeing error... a diabolical disorientation is invading the world, deceiving souls... it is painful to see such great confusion, in so many persons who occupy positions of responsibility... the fact is that the devil has succeeded in bringing in evil under the appearance of good... the Virgin knew that these times of diabolical disorientation were to come". To someone who was questioning her on the content of the Third Secret, Sister Lucia one day replied : "It's in the Gospel and in the Apocalypse, read them", and on another occasion she specified chapters 8 to 13 of the Apocalypse.

The second very important public declaration on the Third Secret is contained in the interview which Cardinal

Ratzinger gave to the journalist Vittorio Messori in August 1984, as reported in the journal Jesus, in an article entitled "Why the faith is in crisis". Referring discreetly to the content of the Third Secret, which he said he has read, the Cardinal mentioned three important elements:

"The dangers threatening the faith", "the importance of the last times", and the fact that the prophecies **"contained in this Third Secret correspond to what Scripture announces"**.

That is why I have consecrated the last two chapters of my book on the Third Secret, firstly to recalling the great teachings of Our Lord, St. Paul and St. John announcing the troubles, the heresy, and finally the great apostasy which will arise in the Church during "the last times", and secondly to drawing out the extraordinary parallel between chapters 8 to 13 of the sacred book of the Apocalypse and the apparitions and prophecy of Fatima. (This study has been issued as a separate pamphlet by Augustine Publishing Company, under the title *Fatima and "the Last Times"*).

So, in conclusion, we can be certain that Our Lady's Secret is clear, and without the slightest ambiguity or difficulty in interpretation. Let us therefore pray unceasingly so that the Holy Father can receive from God the light and the strength which will permit him finally to conquer all obstacles. Is it not normal, is it not now a matter of the utmost urgency to have recourse to the Mother of Perpetual Succour ? For is it not the Immaculate, and "She alone, who can help us", as she herself warned us in her public message of 13 July 1917 ?

BIBLIOGRAPHY

The list which follows is taken from Brother Michel's *Toute la Verité sur Fatima*, and indicates the extent of the author's research on the subject. However, the author states that this is not an exhaustive bibliography but simply a reference to all those works designated in abbreviated form in the footnotes of his three volumes.

Father J.M.Alonso, CMF. (Dd. 12 Dec. 1981)
Ephemerides Mariologicae, the Claretian review of Mariology published from Madrid. He published the following articles in this review , listed by year : 1967, Fatima y la critica, pp. 393-435; 1969, Fatima, proceso diocesano, pp. 279-340; 1972, El Corazon Inmaculado de Maria, pp. 240-303; Chronica, pp. 421-440; 1973, continuation of the same article, pp. 19-75; 1982, De nuevo el Secreto de Fatima, pp. 81-94;

Historia da literatura sobre Fatima, 70pp., Fatima, 1967; Segredo de Fatima, in Fatima 50, 1967, Nos. 1,5,6,7,8; Fatima et le Coeur Immacule de Marie, in the collective work, Marie sous le symbole du Coeur, pp. 25-66, Tequi, 1973; Histoire ancienne et histoire nouvelle de Fatima, in Vraies et fausses apparitions dans l'Eglise, pp.58-99, Lethielleux, 1976; Fatima, historia y mensaje, 94 pp., Centro Mariano, Madrid, (CMM) 1976; La verdad sobre el Secreto de Fatima, 119pp., CMM, 1976; Fatima.Espana.Rusia. 140pp., CMM, 1976; Fatima in Lucia's Own Words, edited by Fr. L.Kondor,SVD, with Foreword, introduction to each memoir, and notes by Fr. Alonso. Imprimatur,1976; La gran promesa del Corazon de Maria en Pontevedra, 79pp., CMM, 1977; Fatima ante la esfinge, 152pp., Sol de Fatima, Madrid, 1979; O Dr. Formigao, 495pp., Fatima, 1979; Fatima, escuela de oracion, 140pp., Sol de Fatima, Madrid, 1980.

Michel Agnellet: Miracles a Fatima, 240pp., Trevise, 1958.

APELO E RESPOSTA : Semana de estudos sobre a mensagem de Fatima, 373pp., Convento dos Capuchinhos, Fatima, 1983.

Jaime Vilalta Berbel: Los Secretos de Fatima, 194pp., Fatima, 1979.

Canon C.Barthas (Dd. 26 Aug. 1973):
Fatima, merveille inouie, 348pp., Fatima-Editions (F-E), 1942; Fatima, merveille du XXe siecle, 359pp., F-E, 1952; Fatima, 1917-1968, 396pp., F-E, 1969; Il etait trois petits enfants, 259pp., Resiac, 1979; Ce que la Vierge nous demande, 227pp.,F-E, 1967; De la grotte au chene-vert, 220pp., Fayard, 1960; Fatima et les destins du monde, 121pp., F-E, 1957; Le message de Fatima, 260pp., F-E, 1971; Les colombes de la Vierge, 164pp., Resiac, 1976.

Abbé Pierre Caillon: La consecration de la Russie aux tres saints Coeurs de Jesus et de Marie, 64pp., Tequi, 1983.

F.Carret-Petit: Notre-Dame du Rosaire de Fatima, 204pp., La Bonne Presse, 1943.

Father J.C.Castelbranco (Dd. 12 Apr. 1962): Le prodige inoui de Fatima, 260pp., Tequi, 1972.

DE PRIMORDIIS CULTUS MARIANI : Acta congressus mariologici-mariani in Lusitania anno 1967 celebrati, 587pp., Rome, 1970.

Father M.Dias Coelho: Exercito Azul de N.S. de Fatima, 60pp., 1956; Nucleo da mensagem de Fatima, article in Apelo e resposta, pp. 151-165; numerous articles in the review Mensagem de Fatima, (see below).

Father Luis Gonzaga da Fonseca, S.J. (Dd. 21 May 1963): Nossa Senhora da Fatima, 414pp., Porto, 1957.

Abbé Jose Geraldes Freire: O Segredo de Fatima, 205pp., Santuario de Fatima, 1978.

Canon José Galamba de Oliveira (Dd. 25 Sept. 1984): Fatima a prova, 134pp., Grafica, Leiria, 1946; Jacinta,

206pp., Grafica, Leiria, 1982.

Mgr. Luciano Guerra: Fatima e a autoridade pontificia, article in De primordiis cultus mariani, pp., 223-256, 1967; Fatima e o Romano Pontifice, article in Apelo e resposta, pp., 21-104, 1983.

John Haffert: Meet the Witnesses, 155pp., AMI Press, Fatima, 1961; Fatima, World Apostolate, AMI Press, 1983.

Francis Johnston: Fatima, the Great Sign, 156pp., Augustine Publishing, Devon, 1980.

Dom Claude Jean-Nesmy, OSB: La verite sur Fatima, 256pp., SOS Editions, 1980.

Father Joao de Marchi, IMC: Era uma senhora mas brilhante que o sol, 320pp., Fatima.

Father Antonio Maria Martins, S.J: Memorias e cartas da Irma Lucia, 472pp., Porto (P), 1973; O segredo de Fatima e o futuro de Portugal, 226pp., P, 1974; Fatima, Documentos, 538pp., P, 1976; Cartas da Irma Lucia, 126pp., P, 1979; Mensagem de Fatima, 70pp., P, 1982; Fatima, caminho de paz, 101pp., P, 1983; Novos documentos de Fatima, 396pp., Loyola, Sao Paulo, 1984; Fatima e o Coracao de Maria, 118pp., Loyola, Sao Paulo, 1984.

Father Sebastiao Martins dos Reis (Dd. 27 Oct. 1984): Fatima a suas provas e o seus problemas, Lisbon (L), 1953; Na orbita de Fatimas, rectificacoes e achegas, 191pp., 1958; As pombas da Virgem de Fatima, 183pp., L, 1963; O milagre do sol e o Segredo de Fatima, Salesianas, Porto (SP), 1966; Sintese critica de Fatima, 187pp., P, 1968; A vidente de Fatima, 132pp., L, 1970; Uma vida ao servico de Fatima, 400pp., P, 1973; Na orbita de Fatima, reaccoes e contrastes, 176pp., SP, 1984.

Mgr. J.J.Mowatt: Russia and Fatima, 40pp., Blue Army, 1956.

Father Hermann Netter, S.V.D: Fatima Chronik (in

German), 40pp., Grafica de Leiria, 1956.

Abbé R.Payriere: Fatima le signe du ciel, 128pp., 1956.

Pope Pius XII: Documents pontificaux de Sa Saintete Pie XII, 1939-1958, Editions Saint-Augustin, Saint Maurice, Switzerland.

G.Renault (Remy): Fatima, illustrated album, 261pp, Plon, 1957; Actualite de Fatima, 173pp., Apostolat des editions, 1970.

Father J.Rolim: Francisco, Florinhas de Fatima, Uniao grafica, 1947.

Father G.Schweigl, S.J.: Fatima e la conversione della Russia, 32pp., Pontificio Collegio Russico, 1956; Immaculatam Cor Mariae et Russia, Pro Patribus Concilii tantum (typewritten text), Rome, 1963.

Father T.Videira, O.P: Pio XII e Fatima, 63pp., Verdade et Vida, 1957.

William Thomas Walsh: Our Lady of Fatima, 238pp., Macmillan, 1947.

REVIEWS

Fatima 50 : Issue No. 1 of 13 May 1967. An illustrated monthly review, edited by Canon Galamba, no longer in print.

The Seers of Fatima. A bulletin to promote the causes of the beatification of Francisco and Jacinta, edited by Father Luis Kondor, S.V.D., Vice-Postulator, Aptdo 6, Rua de S.Pedro 9, P- 2496 Fatima Codex, Portugal.

Mensagem de Fatima. A bi-monthly publication, founded and directed by Father Messias Dias Coelho, Sameice, 6270 Seia, Portugal.

The Fatima Crusader. The official publication of the International Fatima Rosary Crusade, edited by Father Nicholas Gruner from Box 602, Fort Erie, Ontario, Canada, L2A 5X3.

OUR LADY'S APPEAL TO SOULS

The immediate object of Our Lady of Fatima's message is to save sinners from Hell, and to re-kindle the faith and zeal of Christians so that the example of their lives will draw souls to God. She first gave this explicit direction to the seers on 13 July 1917, when she stated: " You have seen Hell where the souls of poor sinners go. To save them, God wishes to establish in the world devotion to my Immaculate Heart. If what I say to you is done, many souls wil be saved and there will be peace..".

If after reading this book you find that you have gained a clearer understanding of the unprecedented supernatural mysteries of Fatima — if your mind has been enlightened, your faith has been strengthened, and your heart has been touched — then, in gratitude for these graces, may we the publishers of this book suggest that you consider whether there is perhaps something more that you could do in your daily life to further the advance of Our Lady's message, either in your personal devotions, or to help others find that light, strength and comfort which Our Lady has brought to you ?

The issues are momentous. For, as Father Alonso explains in his pamphlet, *The Message of Fatima at Pontevedra*, (1974) "it is necessary to insist that the consecration of Russia will only take place as the fruit of the generalised and intense consecration of all the members and all the communities of the Church. That is why — as Pope Pius XII and Pope Paul VI well understood and expressed it — it is necessary to exhort the faithful to **carry out their personal consecration and to live it intensely**. It is that which is the best means of hastening the hour of the triumph of the Immaculate Heart of Mary, and the coming of the kingdom of God on earth" (p. 38).

To that end, we offer the following checklist as a

means of measuring one's personal response to Our Lady's requests :

— Am I seeking to sanctify my life by daily consecrating all my thoughts, words and acts to the Immaculate Heart of Mary ?

— Am I striving to **live** the message of Our Lady of Fatima, day by day ?

— Do I say the rosary **every day**, as requested by Our Lady of Fatima ? Do I try to encourage my family, friends, and neighbours to adopt this practice ?

— Do I strive to practice the Five First Saturdays devotion as requested by Our Lady at Pontevedra on 10 December 1925 ?

— Do I honour Our Lady by putting up a worthy image or picture of her in my house, and by saying my rosary and other devotions to her in front of it ? Do I encourage my family and others in these practices ?

— Do I strive to fulfill and offer up all my daily duties as conscientiously as possible, in a spirit of prayer, penance and reparation ?

— Do I make sacrifices as often as possible, and say, when doing so: "O my Jesus, it is for love of You, for the conversion of sinners, and in reparation for the offences against the Immaculate Heart of Mary" ?

— Do I pray frequently for the Pope and for the hierarchies of the world, that they may be given the grace to fulfill the requests of Our Lady of Fatima ?

— Do I do all I can within my circumstances to disseminate the truth about Fatima, as made known in the books of Sister Lucia, Francis Johnston, Brother Michel and other authorities ?

Please write to us at the address below if you need any further information about Fatima and would like to help us make Our Lady's message more widely known :

AUGUSTINE PUBLISHING CO., CHULMLEIGH, DEVON, EX18 7HL.